The Fells Point Story

The Fells Point Story

by Norman G. Rukert

Published by Bodine & Associates, Inc. • Baltimore, Maryland • 1976

Colonel Edward Fell

Son of William Fell, founder of Fells Point

—Fells Point Historical Society

First Edition/Library of Congress Catalog No. 75-40655 SBN 910254-11-7

Copyright 1976 by Bodine & Associates, Inc. ● Printed in the U. S. A.

The Fells Point Story

Contents

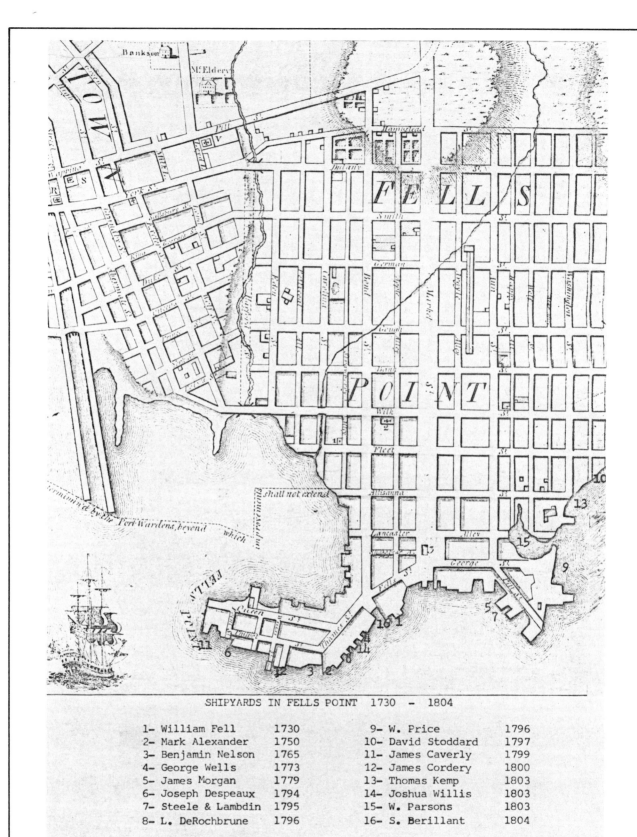

SHIPYARDS IN FELLS POINT 1730 – 1804

1–	William Fell	1730	9–	W. Price	1796
2–	Mark Alexander	1750	10–	David Stoddard	1797
3–	Benjamin Nelson	1765	11–	James Caverly	1799
4–	George Wells	1773	12–	James Cordery	1800
5–	James Morgan	1779	13–	Thomas Kemp	1803
6–	Joseph Despeaux	1794	14–	Joshua Willis	1803
7–	Steele & Lambdin	1795	15–	W. Parsons	1803
8–	L. DeRochbrune	1796	16–	S. Berillant	1804

Fells Point Plat

—Warner & Hanna's Plan of Baltimore 1801

Acknowledgments

Research is based on cooperation and that is what I received the last two years. I have many fond memories and a multitude of obligations for which only brief acknowledgment can be made.

Mary Helen Williams, a young lady whom I predict has a great future in journalism, assisted in the research and editing. She spent many long hours in the Maryland Room of the Enoch Pratt Free Library, the Maryland Historical Society, and the libraries of the *Sunpapers* and the *News American.*

There were many other individuals who helped in the gathering of important information. . . . Robert Eney provided the details on the restoration of the houses in Fells Point. . . . Mrs. A. Murray Fisher who made available several scrapbooks to supply the background of the society's fight against the highway. . . . Dr. Lee Houchins, of Washington, D. C., briefed me on the early trade with Japan. . . . Julia Zarachowicz and James Sadowski, long time residents of Fells Point, supplied the data on life in the Point during the early part of the 19th century.

I am indebted to the Maryland Historical Society, Peale Museum, and the Fells Point Preservation Society who do so much with so little. Dr. F. E. Chatard and Lewis Beck of the Maryland Historical Society shared their time and supplied hard-to-find journals and rare books. Wilbur Hunter, director of Peale Museum, took time out from his busy schedule to assist in selecting pictures from the archives. Robert H. Burgess, curator of exhibits, the Mariners Museum, supplied the pictures and information on the coffee clippers. The Fells Point Preservation Society, especially Margaret Doughtery, John Gleason and Jean Crolius, were most gracious in helping to supply important data on local background and color.

N.G.R.

Anne Bond Fell
The wife and first cousin of Colonel Edward Fell

—Fells Point Historical Society

Illustrations

Prologue

Few people realize Baltimore's importance as a shipping center.
The port today is one of the largest in the
United States handling foreign tonnage. With 4,005
ship arrivals in 1975, Baltimore ranks second in
the handling of containers and the number of man-
hours worked. One out of every 10 jobs in the
state is generated by the port of Baltimore. And
in 1973, the port was responsible for $9.98 of every $100
worth of goods and services produced in Maryland.
What many people don't realize is that
the port, long one of Maryland's greatest assets,
must credit its beginnings to a small community in
Baltimore on the east side of the Patapsco River
called Fells Point.

The Early Years

1730-1799

In the early 1720's, when Edward Fell was preparing to sail to America from England, this country consisted of 12 continental colonies. Georgia, the thirteenth, was not added until more than 40 years later. The population of the East Coast was close to 360,000 and in 50 years that figure would double.

When the first town in Maryland was settled in 1634 one observer described the area as having a genial climate, picturesque landscape and majestic waters. Tobacco was the chief product, and plantations, large and small, were the main feature of the land. Mills and factories were few and export trade was restricted to what each planter could arrange with his native country.

Baltimore County was established in 1659. Its boundaries included what are now Baltimore, Harford and Carroll Counties and portions of Anne Arundel, Howard and Frederick Counties. The population was a scant 2,000 and all of Maryland had only about 12,000.

County residents asked the General Assembly in 1729 to build a town on the Patapsco and the next year Baltimore Town was officially laid out. The population was about 1,000 and growing quickly. Among the many adventuresome people in England the burgeoning colony attracted were the Fells. From what little is known about them it can be assumed that they were ambitious, daring and wealthy men. Two of them, the farseeing brothers, Edward and William, made a rare, dual contribution to Baltimore; they each helped to lay the groundwork for the founding of a town, both of which towns would later be incorporated into the city.

The first Fell to arrive in Baltimore was Edward. He left England around 1726, settled on the east side of the Jones Falls and ran a store on Front Street in what came to be known, partly through his efforts, as Jones Town.

Only a few facts can be found to illuminate his life. One record says that in England in 1725 he appeared at a Quaker meeting house to state his intention of marrying Anne Thomas. (Supposedly, both Edward Fell and his brother William gave up their Quaker faith once they settled in America.) Another account mentions that Edward, after a number of successful years in this country, returned to England and died, leaving his property to his daughter Anne. However, someone else writes that Edward Fell left his holdings to his nephew.

What we do know about him is that he was a shrewd real estate speculator and owned large tracts of land on both sides of the Jones Falls.

One of his more successful endeavors concerned the founding of a new town. In August, 1792 the assembly passed an act to erect a town "on a creek, divided on the east from the town lately laid out in Baltimore County called Baltimore Town, whereon Edward Fell keeps store." It was named Jones Town, after David Jones, the first man to settle the area. Around 1735, after Baltimore Town was started, Jones Town became widely known as Old Town, a name still familiar to many Baltimoreans.

In addition to being credited as one of the first settlers of Jones Town, Edward Fell was evidently prosperous enough to induce his brother William to leave England and try out his luck in America too.

William Fell, also a Quaker by birth and a carpenter by trade, left Lancashire, England in 1730 to sail for Baltimore. Like his brother, he bought large parcels of land in the area including a lot in Jones Town.

In the same year that William arrived in Baltimore, he purchased from Lloyd Harris a 100-acre tract called Copus Harbor, and known at least as far back as 1670 as Long Island Point. Here, in the vicinity of Lancaster Street he erected a mansion and a small shipyard to build two-masted sloops—a humble forerunner to the mighty port Fells Point would become.

William Fell married Sarah Bond in 1732 and they raised their five children, Edward, Ann, Jannet, Margaret and Cathren in the area he had named Fell's Prospect, which due to the contour of the land was frequently called Fells Point. For the next ten years, he continued to buy properties adjacent to Copus Harbor.

By 1745, he owned about 1,100 acres in the Fells Point area. His property was bounded by Chase Street on the north, the waterfront on the south, Patterson Park Avenue on the east and Aisquith Street on the west. He also owned about 300 acres in Anne Arundel County and about 140 elsewhere in Baltimore County.

In 1745, when Jones and Baltimore Towns incorporated to form Baltimore Town, William Fell was named as one of the seven commissioners to oversee the administration of the jurisdiction. He served in this capacity until his death in 1746.

His only son, Edward, inherited most of the estate, including the Copus Harbor tract, the Lancaster Street home and probably the extensive holdings of his uncle Edward, a real estate partner of his brother William, who died in 1738.

Edward married his first cousin, Ann Bond, on November 2, 1758. In 1763 he had the area known as Copus Harbor laid off into a town called Fells Point. Streets had such English names as Thames, Shakespeare and Queen (now Block) and alleys bore such delightful names as Strawberry, Apple, Happy and Petticoat.

The fledgling town got off to a promising start, considering the still-sorry state Baltimore Town was in. Twenty-two years after its charter had been granted, Baltimore Town had about 200 inhabitants; allowing ten people per family, plus slaves, the area could only boast of about 25 to 30 homes, and small ones at that.

A primitive directory compiled in 1752 listed not only the heads of families in Baltimore but also provided some gossipy details on the private lives of the inhabitants, such as "James Long (inn-keeper), Dame Hughes (the only midwife among English folk), Bill Adams (barber), George Strebeck (only wagoner, drove a single team) or Jack Corsby (carpenter)." One wonders how the town residents reacted when the authors of the directory got carried away with their information-dispensing service as in "Philip Littig (whose wife was *accoucheuse* among the German population)."

William Fell
Son of Colonel Edward Fell

As soon as the lots on the Point were designated, Benjamin Griffith bought one on the waterfront and built a wharf and warehouse and Benjamin Nelson, a shipwright, left Cecil County to establish a shipyard on Philpot Street. Other waterfront lots were purchased by Captain Charles Ridgely, George Patton, Isaac Griest and Jesse Hollingsworth, each constructing a wharf or warehouse. The remaining waterfront locations were bought by George Wells, Samuel Purviance, Isaac Van Bibber and William Smith. Many of these men who took the initiative to buy lots in the young town would figure in the later history of Baltimore City. It was during these years, the 1760's, that Fells Point began the growth that 20 years later would make it the center of shipbuilding in Maryland.

The ideal location of the Point, and the proximity of large timber tracts with white oak, locust and red cedar, contributed to the growing shipbuilding industry. Georgia pine, iron manufactured at nearby foundries and naval stores were easily accessible. The labor force swelled when an influx of Acadians settled at Fells Point, many becoming ship carpenters and mariners.

Mark Alexander, of Thames Street east of Caroline; Benjamin Nelson, of Philpot Street and George Wells, of Thames and Bond Streets, were some of the early shipbuilders contributing to the design of the most romantic vessel in United States history—the Baltimore Clipper. Using the Jamaican sloop as a model, the builders made some technical refinements, the most notable of which was the change from sloop to schooner rig. The chief characteristics of the craft were long, light and extremely raking masts, little rigging, low freeboard, great rake to stem and stern posts, with a great deal of drag to the keel, aft. The deadrise was great and bilges slack, beams usually great for their length, nearly always flush-decked. The crafts had wide, clear decks suitable for working the ships and handling the guns. The Baltimore Clipper first received worldwide attention during the Revolutionary War.

Though Edward Fell was occupied with his business and developing the new town he had a minor domestic problem which must have caused him some concern. With the help of his father-in-law, John Bond, he was trying to settle the Fell family estate in England. A friend of Bond's, William Skyrin, a lawyer who lived in England, was handling the selling of the home in Lancaster. After the exchange of several letters Skyrin wrote on February 14, 1766 that the estate had been sold by him "by virtue of a letter of attorney from Edward Fell of Maryland in North America to Roger Fisher of Ulverstone . . . in the manor of Pennington of County Palatine of Lancaster." In March, though, Skyrin wrote that he was having trouble collecting the money. The spate of letters ends here. Whether Edward Fell or another member of the family ever obtained the money is not known. These letters and about 150 other papers of the Fell family have been purchased by the Rukert Corporation. Many of the documents, previously stored in Chicago, will be donated to Maryland museums.

Edward Fell died in 1766 at the age of 33. He was survived by his wife, Ann, and his seven year-old son William, to whom he bequeathed two thirds of his estate. Fell also stipulated in his will that William be "put to the study of law." One of the last records of Fell's life is an account to Adair Dallam, February 19-22, 1766. Fell bought from Adair a lace hat, two yards of linen and a spyglass. He probably wanted the glass to study the increasing numbers of ships coming in and out of the now bustling Fells Point port.

Fells Point, with its deep water, facilities for building and fitting vessels and its number of artisans, had become a rival of Baltimore Town. The Point had grown so much that new settlers had a difficult time deciding whether to live in Baltimore or Fells Point. The wealthy and optimistic bought lots in both.

A good indication of the mounting competition between the expanding towns is an instance that occurred a few months after Fell's death.

Ann Fell, his widow and executrix, placed an ad in the *Maryland Gazette* in which she demanded that those who had purchased lots on the Point pay their debts. Some people had spread rumors that the title to the land was in question, Mrs. Fell said, that the water was bad and the Point an unhealthy place to live. She said she could prove the rumors were unfounded. John Bond, her father, backed up her statement, claiming that the stories had originated with jealous Baltimore landowners, people who wanted to discredit prosperous Fells Point.

Not much more is known about Ann Fell except that she later married James Giles of Harford County and bore him three children, Joanah, Jacob and Susannah.

The customs and manners of Fells Point in the days when Ann and Edward Fell lived in their house on Lancaster Street are well-documented.

The early houses built on lots laid out by Fell were small, wooden ones, one and one-half stories high and about 12-14 feet wide. There were small rooms on the first floor and an attic on the second with a dormer window. The houses had low ceilings, small windows with panes of green glass and whitewashed, not wallpapered, walls. Housewives sprinkled clean, white sand on the floors of their homes.

Furniture was usually made of walnut or mahogany. Pewter dishes were common and a side table would display decanters of Holland gin, Jamaican rum, cognac or Madeira. Beef and poultry were served at most meals. Few vegetables were eaten and milk and tea were the popular beverages.

Women were usually married by the time they were 20. One enamored writer said of the children they "were beautiful to behold, and without the least blemish; bashfulness and modesty in the young were then regarded as virtues." While working, men wore buckskin breeches, checkered shirts, leather aprons and red flannel jackets. One of the favorite recreations, and probably one of the few for the working class, was to dress up in the evening and go to a neighbor's house to chat. Men donned their three-square hats, wigs and coats with large cuffs. Women could usually be seen after dusk wearing a cape and bonnet, and under their dresses, hoops that went from two to six inches on either side.

As the Fells Point population grew, so did the demand for churches.

Bishop Francis Asbury preached the first Methodist sermon in Baltimore at Fells Point in 1772. Shortly after his visit, Messrs. Jesse Hollingsworth, George Wells, Richard Moale and others formed a Methodist society. At first services were held in private homes or in a sail loft at the corner of Wilks and Block Streets. In November, 1773, the group bought a lot at the corner of Fleet Street and Strawberry Alley (now Dallas Street) and built the first meeting house.

Later in the century, other religious faiths would build their churches in the community.

The first issue of the *Maryland Journal and Baltimore Advertiser,* a Baltimore published newspaper, was distributed in Fells Point in 1773. Many of the early papers carried some outrageous news, such as this item:

Baltimore August 18, 1773. Many people in Fells Point having hither neglected to pay their public duty this year, my deputy has my orders to execute every person that has not paid, without distinction, as I am to leave the office in November and all accounts must be settled with J. R. Holliday—Sheriff of Baltimore County.

According to another newspaper ad, indentured servants and adventurers with special qualifications arrived on ships that docked at Fells Point. Two typical advertisements read:

> Just arriving in the ship Neptune, Captain Lambert Wilkens, from London, a number of likely, healthy, indented servants, viz.: Tailors, butchers, barbers, masons, blacksmiths, carpenters, schoolmasters, brass founders, brickmakers, clothiers, clerks watch and clockmakers, weavers, printers, silversmiths, farmers, laborers and several women, viz.: spinsters, Mantuamakers, etc., whose indentures are to be disposed of on reasonable terms by John Cornthwait, James Williamson and the captain on board.

> On board the Neptune, lying at Fells Point—I. Williams, late vinturer in London, who has served as valet de chamber to several noblemen; his last place was that of butler to the Duke of Bolton, and for these few years past kept a large tavern, but through honest principles surrendered his all and was thereby reduced to bankruptcy. He shaves, dresses hair, is thorough master of the wine trade and tavern business, likewise understands brewing and cookery; would willingly engage with any gentleman, hair dresser or tavern keeper. Also a young man who has a college education, would be glad to engage as an usher or private tutor in a gentleman's family; he can teach the minuet, cotillion, etc., and writes all the law hands. Any gentleman wanting such persons, by applying to the above ship within fourteen days from the date thereof, will be treated with on the most reasonable terms.

These two and the indentured servants apparently stayed on board the vessel until their services had been engaged.

The institution of a night watch was tried in 1775. Isaac Van Bibber was in charge of the project which employed two assistants who patrolled the streets from 10 p.m. until dawn, announcing the time every quarter hour. But the system was inefficient and soon discontinued.

During these years, Baltimore Town had pulled ahead in the race. An act was passed in 1768 to erect "a courthouse and public prison for Baltimore County, in the town of Baltimore, and for making sale of the old courthouse and prison." This legislation thus moved the county seat from Joppa to Baltimore. Many date the growing influence of Baltimore from this period, though it still looked little like a city.

A few years later, in 1773, another act passed by the General Assembly again had the effect of diminishing the importance of Fells Point. The legislature annexed about 80 acres of Fells Point to Baltimore Town on the east. More annexations would continue until 1782. Needless to say, Baltimore became more important with the inclusion of much of Fells Point. The ordinance included property along the waterfront north to Fleet Street. One advantage for the Point was the immediate improvements made, such as cobblestoned streets and new bridges.

Soon after the annexation, a census was made of Fells Point. The population was 821. The breakdown included servants, 74; Negroes, 65 and free Negroes, 7. The Point's nickname at this time was Deptford Hundred. Some early authors thought the name was used because of the resemblance the Point bore to a shipping and ship-building center in London.

When the Revolutionary War started, Fells Point was equal to the job that faced it.

The Continental Congress passed the first act for the formation of a navy on October 13, 1775. That same month, the Continental Marine Commission purchased the *Wasp* and the *Hornet,* both of which were armed and fitted at Fells Point. The two ships were the first regular cruisers to go to sea under the new government.

The second officer of the *Hornet* was Joshua Barney, a colorful personality. He was born in Baltimore on July 6, 1759, the seventh of 14 children of Frances and William Barney. Joshua, who seemed to have an inborn passion for the sea, was allowed to leave school at the age of ten. His father, early in the year of 1771, en-trusted him to a Baltimore pilot, under whose supervision he gained valuable expe-rience. The next year he was apprenticed to Captain Thomas Drysdale, his brother-in-law, who commanded a small brig in the Liverpool trade. In January 1775, while on a voyage to Nice with a cargo of wheat the captain died. Since there was no mate, Barney, then just 16, took command. The vessel, in a leaky condition because of continued storms, was taken to Gibraltar. Here Barney successfully nego-tiated a large loan for repairs and proceeded to Nice where he sold his cargo to advantage in spite of the intrigues and extortions of the officials. Returning to America, he took advantage of the opportunity to earn money for his employer by chartering his ship as a transport to the Spanish army. He witnessed the army's defeat at Algiers and afterwards transported some of the defeated troops back to Alicante. Recrossing the Atlantic in October he appeared before his astonished employer who, with diffi-culty, believed his story.

Barney entered the naval service of the colonies that same month. He was assigned to the *Hornet* and one of the his first duties was to recruit a crew. On October 29, the first national ensign arrived in Baltimore from Philadelphia to be flown on the *Hornet*. It was the first flag representing America to be seen in Maryland and the following morning at sunrise, Joshua Barney had the enviable honor of unfurling it to the sound of drums and fifes. The spectacle attracted a crowd of curious people and by that evening Barney had a full crew.

The first cruisers in the navy of the "Thirteen United Colonies" were fitted out, manned and armed in Fells Point, sailed under Maryland officers, and to a great extent, owed their efficiency to the energy and enterprise of her shipbuilders and the patriotism of her citizens. Within four months after the declaration of war the merchants of Baltimore and Fells Point had sent to sea 42 privateers and letters-of-marque, carrying about 330 guns and from 2,800 to 3,000 men.

In the fall of 1775 a report was received that British warships had entered the Chesapeake Bay. The merchants of Baltimore and Fells Point, fearing continued interference in carrying on trade in the Bay, requested the assembly in Annapolis to form a Maryland navy. By December the state had commissioned 25 vessels, consisting of brigs, sloops, galleys and barges. No schooners were taken as they were being used as privateers. The squadron, commanded by Captain James Nicholson, was ordered to protect all shipping on the Chesapeake Bay from Cape Henry to Fells Point.

John Gordon, Robert Dashiell, John Green and William Middleton were among the large number from Fells Point who served as officers in the Maryland navy.

In March 1776 the British sloop *Otter* was reported in the Bay. As she neared the Patapsco River the citizens of Baltimore and Fells Point stretched a chain, supported by 21 small sunken vessels, from Whetstone Point (Fort McHenry) to Lazaretto Point and quickly constructed a series of batteries on Fells Point. The situation was relieved when Captain Nicholson, in the state ship *Defence,* drove the *Otter* out of the Patapsco River.

During December 1775, Congress authorized the building of 13 ships of war. On January 24, 1777 the shipyard of George Wells, Thames and Bond Streets, delivered the *Virginia,* a frigate of 28 guns, the first ship built for the Continental Navy. In April the Marine Committee ordered her to Martinque, though she did not go for lack of a suitable crew. Finally on June 1, the *Virginia,* under the command of James Nicholson, (a better politician than commander) sailed from Fells Point. She proceeded down the Bay as far as York River where she was met by a squadron of British warships and chased back to Fells Point. In January and again in February 1778, the *Virginia* made two other futile attempts to get to sea, ending in the same result—a retreat to Fells Point.

At the end of March, Captain Nicholson made his final attempt to take the frigate to sea with Lt. Joshua Barney now on board as second in command. Everyone was optimistic as a favorable wind drove them down the Bay. The object was to escape through the Capes under the cover of darkness. On the night of the 31st, the *Virginia* was abreast of the Capes when the pilot led her over the middle ground, and she was grounded. With the wind behind her, she beat over the shoal, knocking off her rudder and was forced to anchor.

As dawn broke three British frigates were close by. When Captain Nicholson saw the frigates, he ordered his barge to be lowered, and without an explanation, without waiting even to secure his papers and private codes, he left the *Virginia*. His officers and men were stunned, they could not believe that he was deserting them. He made good his escape to shore.

This left Lt. Barney in command. He gave an order to cut the cable on the rudder, figuring from the direction of the wind that the ship would be driven ashore on Cape Henry, where they could destroy her. This order was never carried out as other officers, in fear of being blown out to sea, opposed him. They insisted on the rule of majority and Barney was forced to give in. The seamen, seeing Barney overruled, gave themselves up for lost. They broke into the slop room and drank as much as they could. Barney spent his time destroying the ship papers and cutting the ropes on the rudder to render the *Virginia* useless to the British.

At ten o'clock the *Virginia* was boarded by a party from the British frigate *Emerald,* commanded by Captain Caldwell. The American prisoners were distributed among the three British ships. Barney was taken aboard the *Emerald,* where Captain Caldwell treated him with respect, even sharing his cabin with the prisoner.

The next day Captain Nicholson came aboard under a flag of truce, and with matchless effrontery inquired about his clothes. At the sight of him, Barney was beside himself. Later he wrote, "I could not help upbraiding him with his conduct in quitting the ship, the first man, when if he had remained on board there was not the least doubt but we should have run the ship ashore where she might have been destroyed, by which means prevented falling into the enemies' hand and saved 300 men from being made Prisoners." Captain Nicholson ignored Barney; gathering his personal effects, he returned to the shore under the flag of truce.

Lt. Barney was put aboard the British frigate *St. Albans* to be taken to New York. During the trip up the coast he plotted with the rest of the prisoners to seize the *St. Albans* and sail it back to the Chesapeake Bay. He almost succeeded but was betrayed by one of the few French prisoners aboard. After five months of captivity he was exchanged for a British officer of equal rank.

Congress investigated the loss of the *Virginia,* but Nicholson escaped court-martial. In the following year he was given command of another of the new frigates, the *Turnbull.* So ended the saga of the ill-fated *Virginia,* the first ship built for the United States Navy, lost without firing a shot.

The incident of Barney and the *Virginia* seemed to stimulate the war effort in Fells Point. Between April 1, 1777 and March 14, 1783, 248 privateers sailed from Baltimore, and most of them were built in Fells Point. Due to the increased demand for rope, used in the rigging of privateers, the first rope walk in Baltimore, a long narrow building for the manufacturing of rope, was erected in Fells Point in 1778 by Lux and Smith near Bond Street.

The Continental Congress met in Baltimore from late December, 1776 to late February, 1777. Samuel Purviance and William Smith, two early landowners in Fells Point, were among the prominent merchants who entertained the delegates in their Baltimore homes. John Adams wrote to his wife about a dinner given by Mr. Purviance, "The guests included John Hancock and lady, the two Colonel Lees and their ladies—a brilliant company."

The war was declared over on April 15, 1783 and four days later Fells Point had a glorious celebration.

One sign that Baltimore and Fells Point were returning to normal following the war was an act passed in 1784 establishing three new markets—at Hanover Street, Harrison Street and Fells Point. The Point's market was built at the foot of Market Street (Broadway) on land donated by William Fell. Construction was completed in 1785, before either of the other two were finished.

William Fell, the only child of Edward Fell, and the sole heir of the Fell family in America, died on October 6, 1786. He was 27 and a bachelor. In compliance with his father's will, William had studied law. He was a staunch patriot and was much interested in the young republic. He served as sheriff of Baltimore during 1780 and two years later was elected state delegate to the assembly in Annapolis.

He lived in a mansion on the east side of Washington Street where he entertained lavishly. On October 22, 1781, Mr. Fell was host for a ball which Lt. Reeves, a naval officer, described: "as the ladies were very agreeable we danced until three o'clock in the morning. The whole company seemed to enjoy themselves and indeed seemed to be carried away beyond themselves on this happy occasion."

One curious footnote to William Fell's brief life is that he was allegedly the first person in town to drive a curricle and pair—a two-wheeled carriage drawn by two horses, side by side.

A few days after William Fell died, this flowery tribute appeared in a Baltimore paper:

On Friday evening last departed this Life in the 27th year of his Age, William

IN MEMORY OF
EDWARD FELL
MARYLAND 1723 FROM LANCASTER, ENGLAND. ACQUIRED LAND.
JONESTOWN. LATER PART OF BALTIMORE TOWN. IMPORTER. DIED 1743.
WILLIAM FELL
BROTHER OF EDWARD. MARYLAND 1730. MARRIED SARAH BOND 1732.
ACQUIRED THOUSAND ACRES CONTAINING FELLS POINT. SHIPBUILDER.
COMMISSIONER OF BALTIMORE TOWN 1745. DIED 1746.
COLONEL EDWARD FELL
SON OF WILLIAM MARRIED ANN BOND 1758. LAID OUT FELLS POINT 1763. DIED 1766.
WILLIAM FELL
SON OF EDWARD AND GRANDSON OF WILLIAM. SHERIFF. DELEGATE TO ASSEMBLY BORN 1759. DIED 1786.

FELL

Fell Family Tomb
1607 Shakespeare Street

—Photograph by Frank Pilachowski

Fell, Esq., and late Proprietor of Fells Point—a respectable Part of this town—A Young Gentleman of Honour and Probity and of an Amiable Disposition, His life, though short, was marked by many acts of Generosity and Humanity. On Sunday Evening his remains were very respectfully deposited in the Family Vault at Fells Point. The pearly drop which indeed it was a luxury to shed, was seen in many a glistening eye over this afflicting occasion. His Friends recounted with grateful Sensibility his Hospitality and Beneficence, while the Poor emphatically blessed his Memory.

His name is last on the family tombstone at 1607 Shakespeare Street. Fell left his estate to his two half sisters, Joanah and Susannah, and his half brother Jacob Giles.

The citizens of Fells Point and Baltimore celebrated Maryland's ratification of the Constitution with a parade which featured a miniature full-rigged ship, mounted on wheels and drawn by four horses. This tiny ship, built in Fells Point, was 15 feet long and named the *Federalist*. A few days after the celebration it was launched in the Patapsco River with the customary ceremony. Captain Joshua Barney sailed the *Federalist* down the Chesapeake Bay and up the Potomac to Mount Vernon. He presented the ship to George Washington as a gift from the merchants and shipowners of Fells Point and Baltimore. It remained there for nearly two months, until it was ripped from its moorings by high winds and sunk. The present is recorded in George Washington's diary for June 9, 1788.

Fells Point was growing rapidly as more ship captains and owners built their homes there. The homes, considerably more substantial than the early houses, were brick, three bays wide and three and a half stories high, with two dormers in the roof. More exterior and interior trim adorned these homes; there were finely carved mantels and elaborate moldings in the chair rails and window trims. Wallpaper replaced the whitewashed walls. The counting rooms or offices usually occupied the first floor; the living area was confined to the upper two floors, with children's and servants' quarters in the attic. With this increase in housing the Deptford Fire Company, the first in Fells Point, was organized in 1792. The engine house was on the northeast corner of Market (now Broadway) and Fleet Streets.

As the Point was briskly evolving from a village into a thriving seaport, customs and manners were uprooted. Men discarded their wigs and women exchanged hoops for layers of petticoats.

Dancing assemblies were popular; no men under 21 nor ladies under 18 were allowed. The minuet was fashionable among most classes though seafarers claimed that a dance called the hipesam was "everything." Numerous shops opened on Market Street, each displaying different insignias. Importers of Irish linen sported a spinning wheel sign and haberdasheries carried a golden umbrella. Shops stocked with seafarers' wares featured woolen hats, wide petticoat breeches, striped shirts, silver brooches and quartered shoes with buckles.

The Point's boom also engendered, in addition to new customs and modes of dress, the construction of another church, the establishment of more newspapers, another school and more civic improvements.

As the Fells Point Methodists had organized a church earlier in the century, so did the Point Catholics in the 1790's. St. Patrick's, the second Catholic church in Baltimore, was built in Fells Point. The Point's Catholics, finding it inconvenient to attend St. Peter's church at Saratoga and Liberty Streets, got permission from Bishop John Carroll (the first bishop of Maryland) to form a parish. The first church, if one may dignify it with a title, was opened by Father M. Antoine Garnier in 1792. It was only a crude, unplastered garret on the third floor of a house standing at the northeast corner of Bond and Fleet Streets, which Father Garnier secured for a nominal rent. In 1792 Bishop Carroll, accompanied by Father Jean M. Tessier (later a Superior of St. Mary's Seminary), celebrated the first Mass in the parish and preached the first sermon. His audience numbered 12. Throughout that year, Father Garnier ministered twice weekly to a growing congregation. Finally, the owner of the building, fearing the continued crowding of the upper floor would cause the building to collapse, requested the congregation to look for other quarters.

In 1793 the second St. Patrick's Church was opened in the home of Edward Hagthrop on Thames Street, between Bond Street and Market (Broadway). In a double parlor on the second floor Father Garnier and Father John Floyd, who succeeded him in 1795, offered Mass and administered the Sacraments. In 1796 the congregation resolved to put an end to these make-shift arrangements. At no time had the accommodations been sufficient to meet the needs of the people and the only practical solution was to strike out for themselves and build a church. Father Floyd, the young pastor, leased a lot 60 by 40 feet on the west side of Apple Alley (Bethel Street), just below Wilks Street (Eastern Avenue), at an annual rate of $40. Here the first building for the exclusive use of the congregation was erected. It was a poor church built by poor people. It was paid for by funds collected by Father Garnier and an agreed assessment on the head of each family of $16, either in cash, materials or labor. Supplementing this were a number of contributions from Protestant neighbors. To make ends meet parishioners gave freely of their time, and many worked long hours by lantern light after toiling all day at their usual occupations.

It was not a church an architect would boast of. The exterior was of brick. The floor space (33 by 40 feet) was disproportionate to the height of the walls (12 feet); the walls were too thin for the roof; the roof (14 feet at its highest point) was too badly arched for either beauty or safety; the work was done too fast (the shingling of the roof only took one day). Parishioners did not wait for the church to be completed. Before the walls were plastered and the floor laid they began to attend services. Ordinary wooden benches were built to accommodate the people, providing a seating capacity for about 300. A wooden altar stood in the midst of the narrow sanctuary. The formal opening of the church took place on June 5, 1797, when Bishop Carroll dedicated it and addressed the congregation.

Fells Point was described this way by a visiting Frenchman in the early 1970's:

Arrived the following morning at the wharf in Baltimore having keenly enjoyed the approach to the town which comes into view by stages gradual enough to continually whet one's curiosity. Especially noticeable is the right side, a section of the town called the Point, with its nicely built new houses, which are growing in numbers, shady walks and English named streets. The harbor at the Point was well filled with boats, ready to sail and flags floating because of Sunday, presented a gay scene.

Nickolas Leeke, a school master in Annapolis, moved to Fells Point in 1794 and opened a school for boys. The wooden building, which housed the school, is still standing on the south side of Aliceanna Street between Broadway and Bethel Street.

One incident that occurred on the Point in the 1790's illustrates the importance of the shipping industry and the energy of some of the Fells Point inhabitants.

In March 1794, Congress declared a 30 day embargo on foreign commerce because of an infringement in neutral waters. The embargo caused consternation in Fells Point; at the end of the 30 days, Captain Ramsdell, whose vessel was docked at Fells Point, lowered his ship's flag to half staff to indicate his displeasure. Captain David Stodder and others, believing this a blasphemous act, seized Captain Ramsdell and a young man named Senton and tarred and feathered them.

Judge Samuel Chase, a Federalist and fiery gentleman, when informed of the incident, issued a warrant for the arrest of Captain Stodder and the other mob ring-leaders. As the prisoners left Fells Point on their way to prison, they were followed by a sympathetic crowd marching to fifes and drums. The crowd's spokesman informed Judge Chase that if the prisoners were sent to jail, the mob would rip down the jail and the judge's house too. Unruffled, the judge gave the prisoners the choice of posting bond or going to jail. Though several in the crowd offered to post bail, the prisoners refused it.

"Then you must go to jail," said Judge Chase. He ordered the sheriff to seize Captain Stodder. The sheriff refused, saying it was more than he could do single-handed. The judge suggested he summon a posse. The sheriff insisted he could get no one to serve on it. "Summon me, sir," the judge proposed. The spokesman of the crowd again intervened, begging the judge to yield to the mob and warning him that his life was in danger. But Judge Chase stood his ground.

"God forbid," he declared, "that my countrymen should ever be guilty of so daring an outrage; but, sir, with the blessing of God, I will do my duty. They may destroy my property, they may pull down my house from over by head, yea they may make a widow of my wife and my children fatherless. The life of one man is a little consequence compared to the prostration of the laws of the land. With the blessing of God, I will do my duty, be the consequences what they may."

The Fells Point mob was no match for such eloquence. Judge Chase relented to the extent of giving the prisoners until the next day to think his offer over. They did change their mind and posted bail the next day. Trial was held a week later—Captain Stodder and the other ringleaders were found guilty, fined and the incident was closed. Judge Chase later was elevated to the Supreme Court.

On March 2, 1795 John W. Allen published the first issue of the *Fells Point Telegraph* on Bond Street, at the cost of $2.50 per annum. The newspaper, published Monday, Wednesday and Friday, contained information about the arrivals and departures of ships and their cargoes. In addition to local news, it carried articles from New York papers, communiques from foreign ports and a bit of poetry. Here are a few items from early editions:

Peculiar character—Jeremiah Kinne, Esq., age 93 years, within the last two months has broke and swinged 291 lbs. of flax. He has 13 children, 85 grand children and 137 great grand children. He made his own coffin some years since and still keeps it in his house.

A hint to bachelors—On Wednesday last, Mr. Busnell Brainard, a bachelor of 62 years of age, was found hanging in his barn. He had been insane by turns for 25 years, otherwise a good moral character.

That the subscriber proposes to open a school the first day of April next, at the Sign of the Swan, on Fells Point, where Mr. Henderson now teaches. Reading, writing, English, grammar, arithmetic, geometry, trigonometry, bookkeeping, surveying and navigation, will be taught. The utmost care will be taken, not only to suppress vice among the pupils, but to excite in them, a love of virtue and morality, which, when united, renders youth amiable, and grey hair venerable.

Municipal improvements made in Fells Point in the waning years of the 18th century included building more wharves, paving the streets and laying out sidewalks, and the town commissioners provided for yet another amenity: "The width of the cellar doors of the old-fashioned porches of front doors (be) limited so that the burghers could not take up too much space allowed for pedestrians, while engaging in their evening chat or pipe before their dwellings."

At the November session of the 1781 assembly, the remainder of Fells Point was annexed to Baltimore Town—from Fleet Street north to Hampstead Street (Fairmount Avenue).

The people who lived on the Point had been fighting the closer and closer ties with Baltimore Town for years and the issue, to jump ahead a few years, came to a climax in 1796.

The residents of Baltimore Town had been contemplating the idea of a city charter for about ten years when in 1793 the legislature passed an act for consideration of such a charter. But Fells Point opposed the idea so vehemently that the plan was dropped. It was not until December 31, 1796 that Baltimore Town finally became a city. But Fells Point didn't give in easily. The demand that the General Assembly had to concede to was that if Baltimore Town incorporated, the people of Fells Point would be exempted from paying any tax toward deepening the upper harbor.

During the post Revolutionary War period, Fells Point shipbuilding boomed. New shipyards were constructed by Steel & Lambdin, Fells Street; William Price, east end of Thames Street; and David Stodder, west side of Harris Creek. Most Fells Point wharves were extended with a new machine capable of driving piles, making it possible to extend them over water as well as land. Richard Parkinson, a New York merchant, during a visit to Fells Point, remarked on the ability to berth vessels of 600 tons in safety, a feat in those days.

A number of refugees, fleeing San Domingo in 1793 because of that country's riots, landed in Fells Point. Two of the immigrants established shipyards at the Point: Joseph Despeaux at Philpot and Point Streets and Louis DeRochbrune, on Thames Street. The waterfront become a forest of spars and canvas as laborers and seamen flocked to the Point. James Armstrong, William Carr, John Fitzgerald and Thomas Green were among a list of people who offered their home to ship officers while their vessels were in port.

As the Point's disparately populated community grew, the area, in the late 1790's, evolved into a rabble-rousing community—red light districts, saloons and dance halls sprung up. By 1796 there were 47 taverns and inns in Fells Point. Some of the more popular ones were Morgan's, Farrell's, O'Neal's and Ryan's. Hamilton

Owens in his book *Baltimore on the Chesapeake* suggests: "Geographically, Fells Point in those days, showed a definite hook point and as the prostitutes took over, one wonders if it is responsible for the term hookers."

In 1794, Congress passed a bill which President Washington signed on March 27 of that year authorizing the construction of six frigates.

The naval captain named by Henry Knox, secretary of war, as captain of one ship was Thomas Truxton, a former successful privateersman during the Revolution. One of his responsibilities was to choose a site on which to build the ship, one of the largest ever to be constructed in the country. He finally selected Stodder's yard on Harris Creek, the eastern boundary of the Point.

The first step was to prepare the yard by laying down gravel and pilings as a base for the vessel. Shortly after this was done at the yard, the plans arrived and the laborers were employed. But building the ship was no easy feat. Months would pass before the shipwrights could locate enough live timber, curved to fit the specifications. Once the timber was procured, however, Truxton and Stodder battled over the design of the vessel. And there were other arguments, delaying the work so much that she was the farthest behind of all the frigates being built.

But finally, on September 7, 1797, the ship was launched and christened the *Constellation*. She sailed from Fells Point on June 26, 1798, the first to put to sea under the bill Congress had passed four years earlier. She was sent to the West Indies to protect U. S. merchant ships from French privateers. After serving for more than 140 years, she was saved from destruction by a group of patriotic Baltimoreans. Now fully restored and an official National Historic Shrine, the *Constellation* is a symbol of American liberty. Some believe her permanent berth should be somewhere in Fells Point, her birthplace.

The U. S. sloop of war *Maryland* with 20 guns, was launched in 1799 at William Price's shipyard at the east end of Thames Street. She was financed by the merchants of Baltimore and Fells Point and presented to the U. S. Government.

The Fells Point port experienced a phenomenal increase in activity during the 1790's. In 1791, 325 vessels arrived from foreign ports and 5,464 bay craft docked there. In 1797 shipping amounted to 59,837 tons, and by 1798 the export cargoes alone amounted to over $121,000,000. The Fells Point shipyards, merchants and shipowners had reason to be optimistic about the future at the close of the 18th century.

Baltimore Clipper

The Golden Years

1800-1859

Some historians consider the first half of the 19th century as the golden age of Baltimore. The city grew and prospered during this time—Baltimore in 1800 had reached a population of 31,514, a 125 per cent increase in ten years, and would, during and after the war years, reap huge fortunes. But Fells Point, though it too would share in the glory, was off to an uneven start.

The principal merchants and traders in the area were beginning to abandon the Point in the early 1800's. Though once it had been convenient and socially proper to live there, recently-arrived immigrants, many finding work in the shipyards building the Baltimore Clippers, drove the wealthier citizens to build new mansions in different parts of the city, notably in and around the Washington monument area. But, the Point was not standing still: new houses went up almost daily and improvements to the wharves and streets were constant. Not only were more homes necessary, but some of the religious groups on the Point were finding that they needed bigger churches, too.

The Methodist congregation, formerly housed at Strawberry Alley and Fleet Street, dedicated a new building at Wilks (Eastern Avenue) and Bethel Streets January 3, 1802. The cornerstone of the new St. Patrick's Church, Broadway and Bank, was laid July 10, 1806. Many felt St. Patrick's was the most imposing church in the city.

An additional fire company, the Fells Point Hose and Suction Company, was organized in 1810 and during that same year, the first bank on the Point, the National Marine Bank, was established. More modes of transportation were developing too. One was a ferry run by Peter Paul to carry passengers from the foot of Broadway to Locust Point. The fare was 12½ cents.

Baltimore, with the significant aid of Fells Point, played a major role in the War of 1812. It was this city that most aroused the ire of the British, and it was on Baltimore that England concentrated its anger. The British army, after burning the White House, was repelled by the combined forces of citizens from Baltimore and Fells Point.

Just before the War of 1812, Admiral Sir John Borlaise Warren, commander-in-chief of the British naval forces on the coast of North America, issued this statement: "In six months after war should exist between the two nations, not a single American flag would be seen on the ocean". But the British press was not that optimistic. On June 10, 1812 this editorial appeared in the London *Statesman*—"They

(Americans) possess nautical knowledge with equal enterprise to ourselves. In a predatory war of commerce, Great Britain would have more to lose than to gain—and what commerce they might have, would be carried on in fast sailing armed ships".

War was declared on June 18, 1812 and within four months, 42 privateers had sailed from Fells Point, carrying 330 guns and 3,000 men. The shipyards of Fells Point had refined the Baltimore Clipper to near perfection, and as a privateer it was without equal. Baltimore and Fells Point took the lead in the building and fitting of privateers and letters-of-marque.

A privateer was a privately-owned vessel, armed and manned at her owner's expense for the purpose of capturing enemy merchant craft in time of war. International law required that she have a commission, or letter-of-marque, from her government, otherwise she would be considered a pirate. To obtain a letter-of-marque a vessel had to be bonded to the government to satisfy any claims that might arise from illegal captures; two bondsmen were needed for each privateer. Theoretically, the privateer had no right to her prizes until they were condemned by due process of law, but as the privateer could destroy vessels at sea, this was a mere formality. The owner, officers and crew held shares in the privateering enterprises. Privateers usually carried two classes of men—the "gentlemen seamen," who came from good families, enjoyed privileges on board and "typical privateers," who were freelance men-of-war. The obvious differences between the two groups generated many clashes and mutinies aboard privateers were frequent.

During the war, 126 privateers operated out of Baltimore, capturing over 500 British ships. Among the most successful privateers were the *Rossie,* which in 45 days took prizes worth over $1,000,000; the *Rolla,* seizing prizes worth over $2,000,000; the *Comet* which captured 35 British ships and, the most famous of all privateers, the *Chasseur,* the "Pride of Baltimore".

Thomas Kemp, who designed and built these four famous privateers, arrived in Fells Point from Talbot County in 1803. He bought property there, including the northeast corner of Market (Broadway) and Lancaster Streets from his father-in-law, John Horstman and the lot bounded by Fleet, Washington and Fountain Streets where he built his shipyard.

Records show that in 1804 when Kemp and his brother built a schooner, their expenses included $62.50 for renting a wharf for three months and $1.75 for the rum used at the launching. A few years later, while repairing a vessel, Kemp paid $3.50 for an anchor and $16.35 for the bowsprit.

In 1807, he began designing and building Baltimore Clippers almost exclusively. For the next nine years, he also made a specialty of making ships faster by adding topmasts, topsail yards and top gallant yards. Kemp's reputation reached an apex in the War of 1812 when the exploits of the *Chasseur, Comet, Rossie* and *Rolla* were known throughout the young republic.

Around 1818, after selling his Fountain Street home, "a very comfortable and roomy two story frame dwelling house, a good brick kitchen and smoke house, a large work shop and very good counting house," as he wrote himself, Kemp retired to Wades Point in Talbot County.

A history of Fells Point would be incomplete without the story of the most famous ship built there. At four o'clock on the afternoon of December 12, 1812, she was launched from the Kemp shipyard. Christened the *Chasseur* and popularly nicknamed "The Pride of Baltimore," this Baltimore Clipper was an inch short of 116 feet long and had a tonnage of 356. The largest craft of her type, she was the second largest private armed vessel to be commissioned at Fells Point and became the area's most celebrated raider.

No picture of her seems to have been preserved, but the following description was penned by an admirer, "She was indeed a fine specimen of naval architecture, and perhaps the most beautiful vessel that ever floated on the ocean. She sat as light and buoyant on the water as a graceful swan, and it required but very little imagination to feel that she was about to leave her watery element, and fly into the clear, blue sky."

Although built for commerce raiding, the *Chasseur* was sent to sea as a letter-of-marque with freight for France by her first owners, the merchant firm of Hollins and McBlair. The owners had hoped that the letter-of-marque would prove more than formal papers. When she neared Annapolis, Captain Durkee found many American vessels anchored in the Severn River, waiting to get by the English fleet blockading the Bay. After making several futile attempts to run the blockade, Captain Durkee decided it was impossible and returned to Baltimore. On September 24, she again sailed for France and once more got no further than Annapolis. After three weeks at anchor, the crew refused to work or even try to sail the schooner to France. Captain Durkee left the vessel and returned to Baltimore to invoke an act of Congress, making the 19 members of the crew who had mutinied subject to a naval court martial. The owners had her return to Fells Point and the mutineers were sent to Fort McHenry to await trial. On November 19, the court martial convened and heard the testimony. The court decided it had no jurisdiction as the *Chasseur* had sailed as a merchant ship and not as a privateer and the Articles of War had not been read to the crew. Captain Durkee's troubles were not over—two of the crew sued him for false arrest and rumors spread along the Fells Point waterfront that he was unqualified to command. He tried to disprove the rumors by placing this advertisement in the *Baltimore American*:

> It appears that some vindictive or slanderous person has taken the liberty to assert in confidence to a certain gentleman, merchant of this city, that my habits of dissipation and drunkenness are such as to render me unworthy of confidence in the transacting of business as a Mariner or Master of a vessel, which has raised a prejudice much to my disadvantage and interest. I therefore invite the mean wretch to come out and substantiate his assertion or give satisfaction, otherwise I shall consider him a dastardly poltroon, not worthy the notice of a highway robber.

Messrs. Hollins and McBlair reached the conclusion that the *Chasseur* was cursed by bad luck. Thomas Kemp, the schooner's builder, was one of a syndicate of 17 men who purchased her when she was put up for auction on November 10. The new owners, bent on privateering, added four long 12 cannon, signed on a new crew of 148 men and procured Captain William Wade as master.

She sailed from Fells Point again on December 26, 1813, on the first of her three-famous cruises. Sailing first to the Caribbean, then across the ocean to the European waters, Captain Wade and his crew captured 11 vessels. He sent six to the United States as prizes, burning the other five at sea. After five months at sea and with his

St. Patrick's Church

The second Catholic Church in Baltimore,
opened in Fells Point in 1792

crew reduced to a minimum, due to the manning of prize vessels, Captain Wade returned to the United States, arriving in New York on June 1, 1814. The first significant voyage of the *Chasseur* had proved profitable for Captain Wade and her owners.

Captain Wade was given his release on June 13 when she was sold at an auction in Baltimore, deliverable in New York. Among the group of Baltimoreans who purchased her was Thomas Boyle, a former master of the Baltimore privateer *Comet*. Captain Boyle, who had just completed a successful cruise on the *Comet* and recognized as a genius in privateering, was selected to command the ship. During that four-month cruise, Captain Boyle and his crew captured 35 vessels with a value of over $2,000,000.

Captain Boyle left for New York to prepare the *Chasseur* for its most famous mission. Ten new long 12 cannon were added, making a total of 16. The captain carried extra spars and canvas so he could alter her appearance to fool both the merchant vessels and enemy warships. Captain Boyle enjoyed a fight.

On July 24, 1814, the *Chasseur* left New York with a hand-picked crew of 150. A man of Captain Boyle's reputation had little difficulty in getting the men he wanted. He decided to carry the war into enemy territory by cruising in the home waters of Great Britain. On the voyage across the Atlantic, she captured five vessels, sending four to the United States as prizes; the fifth was used to send prisoners to England.

As he neared the English Channel, Captain Boyle drew up his bold proclamation of blockade of the United Kingdom. On August 27 he captured the brig *Marquis of Cornwallis* which he decided to use as a cartel, not only for his prisoners, but to carry the document to London to be posted at Lloyd's Coffee House.

The proclamation read:

BY THOMAS BOYLE, ESQUIRE
COMMANDER OF THE PRIVATE ARMED BRIG CHASSEUR

Whereas, it has been customary with the admirals of Great Britain commanding small forces on the coast of the United States, particularly with Sir John Borlaise Warren and Sir Alexander Cochrane to declare the coast of the said United States in a state of strict and rigorous blockade, without possessing the power to justify such a declaration, or stationing an adequate force to command such a blockade.

I do, therefore, by virtue of the power and authority in me vested (possessing sufficient force) declare all the ports, harbors, bays, creeks, rivers, inlets, outlets, island and sea coasts of the United Kingdom of Great Britain and Ireland in a state of strict and rigorous blockade, and I do further declare that I consider the forces under my command adequate to maintain strictly, rigorously and effectually, the said blockade.

And, I do hereby require the respective officers, whether captains or commanding officers, under my command, employed or to be employed on the coast of England, Ireland and Scotland, to pay strict attention to this my proclamation.

And, I hereby caution and forbid the ships and vessels and every nation, in amity and peace with the United States, from entering or attempting to come out of any of the said ports, harbors, bays, creeks, rivers, inlets, outlets, islands, or sea coasts, on or under any pretense whatever; and that no person may plead ignorance of this my proclamation, I have ordered the same to be made public in England.

Given under my hand on board the *Chasseur*.   THOMAS BOYLE
By the command of the commanding Officer
J. B. STANSBURY, SECRETARY

By mid-September, the *Chasseur* posed such a threat to English shipping that the British Admiralty dispatched six fast war vessels to hunt her down. Among the six were the H.B.M. brig *Fly,* H.B.M.S. *Endymion* and H.B.M. brig *Castillian;* each sighted and chased the *Chasseur* without success. For the first time in history, the British were forced to use convoy regulations for linen ships crossing the Irish Sea. Watch towers along the coast were manned to keep a lookout for the Baltimore privateers. The depredations of the American privateers on the coast of Britain had produced so strong a sensation at Lloyd's that it was difficult to get policies underwritten except at enormous rates. Thirteen guineas for 100 pounds sterling was paid to insure vessels crossing the Irish Sea. At Halifax, insurance was refused on most vessels; and on others, 33 per cent was added to the premiums. On September 9, a meeting of the merchants and ship owners was held in Liverpool. A resolution was drawn and presented to the Admiralty that measures be adopted to prevent, as much as possible, the ruinous effect of this "new system of warfare."

During the next two weeks, Captain Boyle and his crew continued to destroy merchant vessels while avoiding British war ships. With his crew reduced to 60 men (a sign of a successful privateer), Captain Boyle decided to head for home. The *Chasseur* arrived in New York on October 24, 1814, with a cargo worth over $100,000 and 48 prisoners. During this cruise, Captain Boyle had captured 14 merchant vessels, but more importantly, had embarrassed the British Admiralty.

During November, she was overhauled, scraped and painted under the supervision of Captain Boyle. Ten of her 16 long 12 cannon were exchanged for carronades, a new, shorter and more effective cannon. A new foremast was installed which carried yards making her a brigantine, though she still carried the necessary equipment to alter her rig.

She sailed from New York on December 24, 1814, on the second cruise under the command of Captain Boyle. Just a few hours earlier at Ghent, Belgium, a treaty of peace had been signed between the United States and Great Britain. The treaty stipulated that prizes taken by either side were valid if captured within 30 days of the ratification of the treaty by Congress and Parliament.

The Captain decided the Caribbean would be a more sensible hunting ground at this time of year. He knew the waters around Great Britain would be closely patrolled and the North Atlantic weather and wind conditions in winter could devastate a crew. The second day out of port, the *Chasseur* ran into a severe gale. Heavy seas pounded the ship and late that afternoon a towering wave carried away the mainmast. Through the night, she was hammered by the winds and seas.

When the gale subsided, the crew spent the next few days repairing the damaged masts and spars under the direction of the ship's carpenter. Captain Boyle held daily drills for his gunners and landsmen.

As the *Chasseur* neared Barbados, a British man of war was sighted outside the harbor of Georgetown. Though he knew he could not defeat the man-of-war, Captain Boyle decided to attack. He had confidence in his crew and felt his ship could outsail any vessel afloat. As he tacked to windward, he had the American flag hoisted, and fired a long 12 at the enemy. The return fire from the man-of-war passed harmlessly over her. For the next hour, Captain Boyle continued his maneuver, keeping out of the range of the enemy guns. The action was observed by some British warships inside the harbor of Georgetown and the commander of the fleet dispatched two men-of-war to help capture the *Chasseur*. Meanwhile, Captain Boyle had sighted a schooner near the shoreline trying to make port and, disregarding the three British warships, immediately gave chase. She quickly overtook the little trader, removed its crew and placed an officer and three men aboard to search for valuables. Captain Boyle took the schooner in tow and made off with the three men-of-war in close pursuit. When she had drawn clear of the warships, the schooner was set afire and cast adrift.

The mainmast, which had been damaged and repaired during the early part of the cruise, needed more repair. Captain Boyle sailed to St. Pierre, a neutral port, to have the work done. Just outside the port, the *Chasseur* captured and sank two coastal schooners. When the repairs were completed, the privateer continued to hunt for enemy ships.

On January 30, she was sighted by H.B.M.S. *Barrosa,* one of the fastest frigates in the Royal Navy. It was a day of heavy squalls and high seas, an advantage for the larger man-of-war. The *Barrosa* continued to gain on her and soon opened fire with her bow guns. Undaunted, Captain Boyle ordered ten carronades and the extra spars to be thrown overboard and placed two long twelves aft. As soon as they were in position, the crew commenced firing at the frigate's rigging. Late that afternoon, the seas began to calm and a shot from one of the twelves hit the top sail of the *Barrosa* enabling the *Chasseur* to draw away. A few days later, she captured the *Corunna,* an armed schooner. Captain Boyle transferred the ship's eight nine-pound carronades to his deck and sent the *Corunna* in with a prize crew. During the next week, the *Chasseur* captured three more vessels, sending two to the United States with crews and burning the third at sea.

On February 21, Captain Boyle sighted a large convoy and for the next five days, he followed at close range hoping to capture any stragglers. At dawn, on Monday, February 26, the lookout reported two sails to the windward, and she left the convoy to investigate. The nearer of the two ships was quickly overtaken and when hailed by Captain Boyle, hoisted the Russian flag. After a boarding party found her papers in order, the ship was released and the *Chasseur* hoisted sails to pursue the other one.

Captain Boyle saw the second ship was a topsail schooner running before the wind with everything set. As the coast of Cuba was nearby, he decided she was sailing for the safety of Havana. As the *Chasseur* drew closer, Captain Boyle, believing the schooner would not offer any resistance, did not clear his deck, but took the precaution of having his guns manned. When Boyle was within 100 yards, the schooner fired a stern gun and raised the English flag. As the privateer drew closer, the American seamen made ready to board. Then the English schooner opened ten gun ports and fired a broadside. The American ship reeled under the impact and through the cloud of smoke, Captain Boyle could see the deck of the schooner swarming with men who were already reloading their guns. This was not just a coaster, but an English man-of-war. Caught completely unaware by the attack, the Americans fought back with deadly effect. The hours Captain Boyle had drilled his crew paid off with dividends. Everyone knew his job and each man performed efficiently. The *Chasseur's* own broadside followed immediately and the marines opened a steady fire with their muskets. For a short time the two vessels were separated by only ten yards. Men fell on both sides, ropes parted and sails were torn to shreds by the heavy

Wildey Monument
Erected to honor the memory of Thomas Wildey, founder
of the first Odd Fellows Lodge in America

fire. The noise was deafening as the cannon roared and the air was filled with smoke and debris. Captain Boyle, wounded by a splinter in the upper arm, directed the fight alongside the helmsman. He was convinced the only way to end the fighting was by boarding. He ordered the helmsman to steer in closer and as the bow of the *Chasseur* touched the schooner's side, Mr. Christie, a prize master, leaped onto the enemy's deck. At the same moment her flag fluttered down she had captured H.B.M. *St. Lawrence,* commanded by Lt. James Gordon. The *St. Lawrence* was formerly the privateer *Atlas* of Philadelphia which had been built on the Chesapeake Bay.

Despite the intensity of the battle, casualties were low on both sides. The *St. Lawrence* reported 15 dead and 25 wounded. Captain Boyle's casualties were five dead and eight wounded. When the American surgeon had treated the wounded aboard the *Chasseur,* Captain Boyle sent him over to the injured Englishmen and ordered supplies and clothing to be sent aboard.

Lt. Gordon requested that the *St. Lawrence* be allowed to carry the wounded to Havana, assuring Captain Boyle that the British would make no attempt to recapture the ship, and it would then be turned over to Boyle's representative. As soon as the wounded had been cared for, the American commander ordered all hands to start repairing the damages to both ships. After the temporary repairs had been made on the *St. Lawrence,* the schooner was made ready for the trip to Havana with Mr. Rapp on board as prizemaster. As the vessels parted, Lt. Gordon thanked the American captain for his kindness and presented him with the following letter:

> To the Captain or Commander of any British ship of war who may capture the *Chasseur* or whatever vessel Captain Boyle commands.
>
> In the event of Captain Boyle's becoming a prisoner of war to any British cruiser, I consider it a tribute to his humane and generous treatment, to state that his obliging attention and watchful solicitude to preserve our effects, and render us comfortable during the short time we were in his possession, were such as justly entitle him to the indulgence and respect of every British subject. I also certify that his endeavors to render us comfortable and to secure our property, were carefully seconded by all his officers who did their utmost to that effect.
>
> J. C. Gordon
> Lieutenant

The story of the *St. Lawrence* was not over. Just outside of Havana, she was stopped by an English warship. Lt. Gordon explained to the captain that the schooner was a prize of the *Chasseur* and said he had given his word that the ship would be turned over to the prizemaster after the wounded had been landed. The captain disagreed and compelled the prizemaster to release the *St. Lawrence.* The vessel was taken to Bermuda for the court to decide ownership. That summer, the court ordered the ship to be returned to the United States to be sold for the account of the *Chasseur.* It was a rare court that would sit in judgment on one of its own vessels and then order her given to a late enemy.

For the next two weeks the *Chasseur* cruised in a leisurely fashion while further repairs were made. On March 15, the brig *Eliza* was stopped and boarded and Captain Boyle was informed that the Treaty of Peace had been signed by the president on

February 17. With the war over, Captain Boyle sailed for home and three days later was in Baltimore.

When the ship passed Fort McHenry, Captain Boyle ordered a salute fired—it was returned by cheers of thousands who lined both sides of the Patapsco River.

As the privateer docked at Fells Point, she was greeted by another crowd which included prominent Baltimoreans. Two weeks later a reception was held in Fells Point honoring Captain Boyle and his crew. If Captain Boyle and the *Comet* were the epitome of privateering, Boyle and the *Chasseur* were its apotheosis.

When the British invaded North Point on September 12, 1814, it was Fells Point and Baltimore—"the den of pirates"—they sought to destroy. The success of the Baltimore Clipper privateers in hampering British shipping had focused attention of the British leaders on Fells Point's shipyards and warehouses. Baltimore, or "Mobtown," as the British press called it, had done more to stimulate the war effort than any other American city.

As the British advanced towards Baltimore, Fells Point merchants, shipwrights and seamen rushed to Hampstead Hill (Patterson Park) to erect a breastwork and battery for the city's defense.

One of the seafaring men who worked on the breastwork was Captain Henry Dashiell, the son of Thomas and Jane (Renshaw) Dashiell. His ancestors were Huguenots and the name of the family is said to have its origin in a pious Huguenot motto: God, a shield.

Henry Dashiell went to sea at an early age and was commander of a ship when he was 21. At 27, Dashiell, a native of Scotland, was master of the *Venus* and sailed for a firm with offices in England and America. He settled in Fells Point in 1799 when he married Mary Leeke.

He was a successful privateer during the War of 1812 and accumulated a fortune. He built a large home at the southwest corner of Aliceanna Street and Broadway where he lived with his wife and nine children.

On September 16, after the defeat of the British troops at North Point and their unsuccessful bombardment of Fort McHenry, Fells Point had a wild celebration. The patriotic spirit prevalent on the Point during the War of 1812 was as strong 40 years later, as illustrated by this entry in the diary of Captain Dashiell's daughter, Alice Ann, in 1852: "September 12, the chivalric blood thrills through my veins on every return of this anniversary."

The captains of the British warships had been amazed by the speed and the handling ability of the Baltimore Clippers. Captain Wise, commander of a British frigate, said to George Coggeshall, an American prisoner:

> "Coggeshall, you Americans are a singular people as it respects seamanship and enterprise. In England, we cannot build such vessels as your Baltimore Clippers; we have no such models, and even if we had them, they would be of no service to us, for we never would sail them as you do. We are afraid of their long masts and heavy spars, and soon would cut down and reduce them to our standard. We strengthen them, put up bulkheads, after which they would lose their sailing qualities, and are of no further service as cruising vessels."

At the end of the hostilities, the British Admiralty, still intrigued by the

Baltimore Clipper, sent Lt. F. F. de Rose to visit the Fells Point shipyards. The builders, though proud of their secrets, would not reveal any of their plans to the English officer.

One of the most appropriate descriptions of a Baltimore Clipper was made by Edward J. Trelawney, English author and adventurer, when he said:

> "A beautiful vessel, long, low in the water, with lofty raking mast, which tapered away until they were almost too fine to be distinguished. I thought there was nothing so beautiful as the arrowy sharpness of her bow and the gradually receding fineness of her quarters. She looked and moved like an Arab horse in the desert and was so obedient to command."

The swiftness of the ship was demonstrated by the *John Gilpin,* one of the fastest vessels ever built. On one of its voyages, she covered 34,920 miles at an average rate of over 183 miles per day. For the 228,553 miles she logged in seven years, she had a daily average of 159 nautical miles.

With no war waging, Baltimore was not as prosperous a city and activity in Fells Point especially slackened off. The shipyards and sailors were idle because, in addition to the end of wartime business, both the flour and tobacco trades were curtailed as a result of competition from other areas. Despite the work slowdown, at least for the shipbuilders and other maritime employees, life in Fells Point went on much as before.

In June, 1815, the first free school in Baltimore was opened on the Point by St. Patrick's Church. Father John Francis Moranville organized a group of parish women under the name St. Patrick's Benevolent Society to help with the school. A month after it had opened, Father Moranville wrote a note to a friend in Emmitsburg describing his efforts: "I have opened a little charity school. We have 50 girls, many of whom know quite *que vous*. We expect that God will grant us success." Peggy James was the first school mistress and the curriculum included subjects usually taught in high school, algebra, geometry and bookkeeping. The school admitted poor children of all races and religions.

When Father Moranville arrived in Baltimore from France in 1794, he was destitute and had to leave his trunk with the ship's captain until he could borrow money from colleagues at St. Mary's Seminary to pay the freight charges. To learn English and earn money, he taught French at a fashionable girls school run by a Madame Lacomb at 36 South Street. He also began saying Mass at St. Patrick's eight times a week. In 1804 he became pastor of the church and one of his first acts was to choose a new site for the church and solicit the funds to build. He was known to distribute his clothes and his wood to the poor; one year he returned a third of his salary to the church.

Some members of the congregation were as generous as he was. A sailor who had won a large sum in a lottery turned his winnings over to the pastor who used the money to buy a lot for the new presbytery and to help yellow fever sufferers.

The pastor himself contracted the fever three times and his parishioners raised money to send him back to France to recuperate, keeping the money from him until he was aboard ship for fear he would spend it on others. He never returned to Fells Point, dying in Amiens in 1824. Before his death, he sent $129, the only money he had left, to St. Patrick's for vestments and an altar ornament.

Broadway

After many years of indecision, the public school system in Baltimore was established in 1826. On February 28, the General Assembly passed an act for the establishment of primary schools in Maryland. It was not until March 8, 1828, that the City Council passed an ordinance creating a board of commissioners with the power to establish schools. After a year's delay, the board decided to establish four schools (two for males and two for females), one of each in the western section of the city and the other two in the eastern section. On September 28, 1829, the first two public schools in Fells Point were opened on Bond Street near Canton Avenue under the direction of Thomas and Harriet D. Randolph. This was seven days after the first school in Baltimore had opened in the basement of the Presbyterian church on the east side of Eutaw Street between Saratoga and Mulberry Streets.

Through the efforts of Thomas Wildey, the first Odd Fellows' Lodge in America, Washington Lodge No. 1, was organized in Fells Point on April 13, 1819. On February 1, 1820, it received a charter from the Duke of York's Lodge at Preston, Lancashire, England. Mr. Wildey, "the Father of Odd-Fellowship in the United States," died on October 18, 1861 at the age of 80. The Wildey Monument on Broadway, north of Baltimore Street, was dedicated a few years later.

According to some reports, the Irish were beginning to be feared in Fells Point, perhaps because their numbers and influence were growing. This incident illustrates some of the tension that must have been felt between the original inhabitants and the Irish new-comers.

In the early morning of March 24, 1819, word reached Fells Point that an effigy of the patron saint of the Irish Catholics, St. Patrick, was hanging from the yardarm of a schooner docked at Spear's Wharf. Quickly an angry mob of Irish laborers from the Point assembled and, without asking questions, began to wreck the schooner. Judge McMechen, when informed of the riot, rushed to the wharf, gathering a number of citizens and peace officers on the way. The incensed Irishmen turned on him and his supporters. At that moment, the mayor, the collector of the Port, and more officials arrived and dispersed the mob. The ringleaders were apprehended and jailed at the next session of the city court.

In addition to being the site of the original free school in Baltimore, the Point was also the scene of another first.

The summer of 1819 in Fells Point was unusually dry and sultry. In late July, a few cases of yellow fever were reported on the outskirts of the Point, particularly along the river in the Canton area. On August 17, the Health Office reported that a number of yellow fever cases has been found on Wolfe Street, near the waterfront, but assured the public that no alarming increase had taken place. For a few days the fever confined its ravages to the wharf area at the far end of the Point and the adjoining streets, Pitt and Wolfe. But by August 27, it had spread to such an extent there was little hope it could be checked before cold weather. The crews of the vessels docked there had been exposed to the fever so police ordered the ships to be moved to a river anchorage. During the first week of September, the disease spread through the entire Point. Everyone who could moved from the area, there was no escape from the fever but flight. At night the area was illuminated by numerous bonfires which were built with the mistaken notion they would purify the air. During the day the Point was almost deserted. About the only movement on the street was a doctor making his lonesome round of duty or a hearse on the way to a cemetery.

A letter written by a young woman to a friend in Philadelphia captures the misery of that time:

"I suppose you have been informed of Elener Dashield's death. She was one of the first that died on the Point this season with the fever. Oh, they say the Point looks awful, scarcely anything to be seen but funerals . . . The town is very unhealthy about the wharves . . . The fever commenced this season on Captain Chase's wharf or thereabouts. He lost two of his daughters. They say there was some old water casks that came out of a privateer put on that wharf as it was about that time the fever broke out. The water casks were very offensive and all around that part of the Point has been very sickly up to Bond Street, and then spread."

Another story indicates how fast the infection could spread: Among the passengers on the ship *Ceres* sailing for Liverpool on September 25 were a gentleman, his wife and their daughter who had lived in a healthy spot in the western part of the city. They rode to Wirgman's wharf to embark. As the ship had already left the dock, the agents had a rowboat waiting for them. The only time they were in Fells Point during the epidemic was when they walked from the carriage to the rowboat, which left immediately. The third day after the ship sailed the young girl was seized with the symptoms of yellow fever and died within a few hours.

During September of that year, 640 cases of yellow fever were reported to the board of health. Two hundred and forty persons died.

On September 22, a decided change in the weather took place after a long and violent northeast storm. The first effects were unfavorable. The number of new cases and deaths suddenly increased to an alarming degree. This continued for a few days, then the number declined. It was not until after October 25 that it was considered safe for the inhabitants to return to their homes.

In 1819 work in the shipyards came to a halt because of the depression following the war. Inflation, the yellow fever epidemic and an abundance of Baltimore Clippers took a toll. Some desperate shipyards, unable to resist the chance for a profit, converted the Baltimore Clippers into ships suitable for the slave trade. Everything was sacrificed for speed; the lines of the ships were sharpened, the spars lengthened and sails added. Though the federal government tried to intervene, the Fells Point shipyards continued the conversion for a number of years. It was a sad ending for so noble a vessel which twice had played a major role in winning and preserving our independence. Howard Chapelle, a well-known maritime author, has written: "Sired by war, mothered by privateering and piracy, and nursed by cruelty, nevertheless, the Baltimore Clipper will always remain the type representative of the highest development of small sailing craft built by American builders." The Baltimore Clipper had established the reputation of the Fells Point shipyards as being among the finest in the land.

In the spring of 1823, a group of Fells Point citizens met and formed the Seamen's Union Bethel Society to serve the spiritual needs of seafarers. The first services were held in a small room in Captain Frazier's house at 41 Fleet Street. Through an act of the legislature in 1825, they obtained a lot on Philpot Street where a small church was erected. The Rev. Stephen Williams was elected chaplain. A larger church was built in 1868 at 1620 Aliceanna Street where is now stands abandoned.

A little known sidelight of Fells Point history is that Frederick Douglass, who became an outstanding American, spent nine years of his childhood on the Point. He was sent there in 1825 from the Eastern Shore at the age of eight to work as a house-boy in the home of Hugh Auld on Aliceanna Street, near Durham. He lived there for seven years and during that time he taught himself to read and write. The ex-slave became an active abolitionist, orator, educator and U. S. Ambassador to Haiti.

It took the Point only a few years to recover from the yellow fever epidemic. When General Lafayette visited Baltimore on October 7, 1824, the Point was back to its usual celebratory self and enthusiastically welcomed the French general. And on July 4, 1828, in honor of the beginning of the B & O, the first railroad in the United States, a parade formed at the foot of Bond Street and marched through the neighborhood.

One of the first ads in Baltimore for pleasure crafts was placed in the *Baltimore American* in 1824 by a Fells Point businessman who ran this notice:

PLEASURE BOATS

The subscriber presents his compliments to his customers and the public for the liberal encouragement received last year, and informs them that he means to continue to furnish PLEASURE BOATS of the first quality for boarding vessels, or for excursions of pleasure any where this side of Annapolis on the shortest notice. He will also, within the above mentioned limits, go up and across the bay, and in conclusion will go to the Fish House, Fort, Lazaretto, or Capt. Melvin's—Apply to near Capt. Case's wharf, No. 1, the corner of Philpot and Thames Streets Fells Point, to   JILES WILLIAMS

As the day of any launching of a ship neared, the excitement in Fells Point was intense. Thousands of Baltimoreans would gather at the shipyard to celebrate. One such launching occurred on May 12, 1826 when a 64-gunship for Brazil was launched at James Beacham's shipyard at the foot of Lancaster Street. A newspaper estimated 40,000 persons witnessed the event (probably an exaggeration as the population of Baltimore was about 75,000). At the conclusion of the ceremonies the owners and builders went to the Shite Hall tavern to drink to the success of the ship. A dinner was served which featured ham, turkey, terrapin and oysters, topped off with goblets of sangaree.

By 1828 Baltimore was on the way to recovery from the depression. At Fells Point signs of life were stirring in the long-idle shipyards. The air was filled with the smells of tar, paint and oakum. The sound of ringing hammers and creaking tackles was heard throughout the Point as yards were reactivated. The increase in activity is described in this letter written by a visitor during that summer:

"We have not been more pleased for a long time, than during a walk through Fells Point on Thursday last. For several years, we have not seen or heard there so much hammering, sawing, etc. The ship carpenters, ship-joiners, blacksmiths and, indeed, the people of every trade are as busy as we ever saw them—the yard shops are filled with cheerful men, and the hum of industry continuously greets the ear. The countenances of the citizens—nay, the very appearance of the houses and streets, have delightfully changed. Three or

Ann McKim

The first clipper constructed in Fells Point in the
1830's for Isaac McKim, a Baltimore merchant

four years ago, we never left the Point without gloomy feelings and a deep sympathy for that valuable class of fellow citizens located there with a sense of the injured that resulted from the depreciated value of property, etc., and perhaps without seeing one new building going up but we returned from our late visit with joy, not altogether mixed with some mortification, that we have not before observed the happy change that had taken place. We have seen, years ago, much more bustle on the Point, but doubt whether ever more real and solid business was doing there at the present time. Our visit was also agreeable because of this occurance. When at one station viewing a large number of busy laborers and expressing our pleasure at the sight one of the most respectable shipmasters of the Point, participating in our feelings said, "Such is the result of the American system."

With the return of prosperity, Baltimore, as one citizen wrote, settled into "a drowsy condition of respectability." An example of the city's newly acquired sophistication was expressed by the same writer: ". . . although Baltimore has the credit of having been the first to introduce gas into use, in its present shape there was nothing in the appearance of the primitive establishment to attract admiration or suggest imitation."

Life "was on a simpler, easier and more natural footing than it afterwards became . . . and that strife had not yet arisen in which victory consists in outdoing your neighbor in dress and equipage," said one resident of early Baltimore.

Indeed the city must have been quite provincial if even "an occasional whirl in what was called a Spanish dance was regarded as of doubtful propriety." And yet maybe Baltimore made up for some of its stuffiness in having, as one person wrote, "intelligence and refinement."

In the Baltimore of 1824, a wealthy man was one who earned a salary of $3,000 a year; the new president of the B & O Railroad, it was rumored, was offered $4,000.

In 1832, The Improved Order of Red Men, an offshoot of the patriotic group, the Sons of Liberty, was organized in Fells Point. According to one source, who called the order the oldest purely fraternal group in the country, it was a social society and the men held their meetings in a tavern on Bond Street. The motto was "Freedom, Friendship and Charity." Shortly after the society was organized, there were internal problems. George Peters, later P. G. Inchones of the I. O. of Red Men, "determined to organize a new tribe and eliminate the objectionable features of the existing society." In 1833 the new group met at Snike's Temperance House on Thames Street and called themselves "children of the forest, who perform the war dance and imitate other Indian manners." The warfare between the two tribes did not last long. They buried the hatchet and smoked the peace pipe when they assembled in 1842 for an anniversary celebration at the "wigwam" of the Lagan tribe in McPherson's Gardens, Bond and Lancaster Streets.

The Police Department of Baltimore built a watch house (station) in Fells Point at the corner of Market (Broadway) and Aliceanna Street about this time. The watch house was manned by two captains, two lieutenants and 12 patrolmen. Anyone arrested would be confined in the watch house until tried by the Justice of the Night Watch. The salaries were captain, $30 per month, lieutenants, $20, patrolmen, $25 and justices, $100.

General John Stricker
A coffee bark built in Fells Point

The Union Coffee House, the first in Fells Point, was opened by Willard Post at the corner of Thames and Market (Broadway) Streets. At the same time the Washington Arcade was built by Joseph Jones on the east side of the market.

During this period the intercoastal trade was carried on by over 2,000 small sailing craft. From northern ports they would bring dried and salted fish, rum, lamp oil, candles, glassware, cheese, potatoes, onions and cotton goods. On the return trip the craft would be loaded with flour, whiskey, yellow corn and leaf tobacco. Commodities from the South included shingles, staves, boards of oak and cedar, timber for the construction of vessels, pitch, tar and cotton. In return they would take whiskey, gin, white corn, hams and European goods.

With an average depth of 16 feet, the docks at the Point could accommodate vessels loaded with 600 tons of cargo with ease. From the western end of Fells Point to the head of the basin in Baltimore, the depth of water diminished to eight feet.

Of great significance in the history of Point shipbuilding was the launching of the *Ann McKim* on June 4, 1833. Built by Kennard & Williamson at Philpot and Point Street for Isaac McKim, a Baltimore merchant, she rapidly became one of the most talked about of American sailing vessels. She was the forerunner of the illustrious fleet destined to make the American merchant marine known in every part of the globe. McKim had her designed with little regard to cost. She was remarkably handsome, constructed of the finest material with sparkling brass guns and fittings and carrying three skysails yards and royal studding sails.

This item appeared in the *Baltimore Republican and Commercial Advertiser* just before the launching:

"We had the pleasure on Saturday last of examining the most masterly and beautiful specimen of naval architecture which has perhaps ever been produced at the shipyards of this or any other city in the United States. We allude to the *Ann McKim,* a ship of nearly five hundred tons burthen, constructed by Messrs. Kennard and Williamson for Isaac McKim, Esq. This noble vessel, now on the stocks and ready for launching, measures from the stem to the taffrail one hundred and forty-three feet, and is copper fastened throughout, upwards of 34,000 pounds of copper bolts and spikes having been used in the bends, sides and deck. The timber composing her frame has been carefully selected from the shipyards of the neighboring cities, where the proper descriptions could not be procured at home, and in her construction she combines all the properties of a first rate ship, strength, capacity, swiftness and beauty of model. The stern is greatly admired for its beauty and the carved devices are handsomely executed. In minutely examining the various parts of this fine ship, the most unskilled in nautical matters will readily notice the masterly style of finish apparent in every part, whether the eye ranges along the protracted length of the deck, or rests upon the beautiful and solid workmanship of everything around. Unlimited by their munificent employer as to cost of the materials, the builders will send forth a vessel which will greatly increase the already extended reputation of the shipwrights of Fells Point. The *Ann McKim* will be launched tomorrow afternoon at half past four o'clock. We omitted to state that the ship has her lower mast in, and is partly rigged."

Fells Point at the height of the coffee trade

And on the day after the launching:

> "The superb ship *Ann McKim* was, agreeably to appointment, launched from the shipyard of Messrs. Kennard and Williamson, yesterday afternoon. The concourse of spectators, both ladies and gentlemen, was immense, and the ship glided off in the most delightful manner, without being attended with any accident, or anything to mar the gratification which the scene afforded."

Contrary to popular opinion, the *Ann McKim* was not the product of a single revolutionary genius, but the climax of long development. Comparison of her drawings with those of earlier ships shows a striking similarity of ideas. She was an extreme design having greater drag to her keel and more exaggerated lines.

The *Ann McKim* sailed in the China trade for a number of years, and upon the death of Mr. McKim in 1837, was purchased by Howland & Aspinwall of New York. The vessel was not the first in the Clipper ship era and it did not directly influence shipbuilders, since no other ship was built like her. But it may have suggested the Clipper design in vessels of ship rig, and passing into the hand of Howland & Aspinwall, it undoubtedly hastened the opening of that era, as the first really extreme Clipper ship, the *Rainbow,* was owned by that firm.

Though the shipyards in Fells Point specialized in building sailing vessels, they also built a number of steamboats. In 1829 the *Pocahontas* was built by Beacham & Gardner, east end of Lancaster Street, for the Elk-River-Baltimore route.

The *Isabel,* the first ocean steamboat to be constructed in Baltimore, was built in 1848 by Levin H. Duncan (or Dunkin) at Thames and Wolf Streets. She was named after the then queen of Spain and her advanced design attracted wide attention and approval. It had a paddle wheel, a hull of wood and was 200 feet long. Her engine was supplied by Charles Reeder's Marine Engine & Iron Works of Baltimore. The *Isabel* was a jinxed steamer from the day she slid into the Patapsco River. Due to a freak accident, four men were killed and 30 injured during the launching on August 5. She was owned by M. C. Mordecai & Co., and operated in the New York, Charleston and Havana run for the next 13 years.

At the outbreak of the Civil War the *Isabel,* while loading cargo at a dock in Charleston, was taken over by the local authorities and transferred to the Confederate government. When the Union navy blockaded the southern ports the *Isabel* was converted into a blockade runner and renamed *Ella Warley.* After a number of successful runs through the blockade she was captured on April 25, 1862 by the USS *Santiago De Cuba* and sent to New York. After the prize court proceedings she was sold to F. W. Reynolds & Co., of Providence, R. I.

On February 9, 1863 she sailed from New York for New Orleans with a cargo of dry goods and leather valued at $175,000. That night, due to a mix-up in signals, the *Ella Warley* was rammed by the steamer *North Star* just forward of the starboard paddle wheel, crushing the starboard boiler. The four men on watch in the boiler room were killed by the escaping steam. She sank in ten minutes but in that short time, the port lifeboats had been lowered and everyone, including 18 women and children, was saved.

With the growth of the railroads, several of the shipyards were given orders for car ferries. The first one to be delivered was the *Susquehanna* built in 1836 by Williamson and Richardson's shipyard on Philpot Street for the Philadelphia, Wilmington and Baltimore Railroad. This ferry was used to transfer passengers across the Susquehanna River from Perryville to Havre de Grace. The passengers were required to disembark from the cars and proceed to the ferry on foot, then walk to the waiting train at the opposite shore; the upper deck of the boat was laid with a track for the transfer of the baggage cars. This probably was the first car ferry used in the United States.

Public transportation came to Fells Point in 1844 with an omnibus line that ran from Franklin and Eutaw Streets to Broadway and Thames. This was a large, four-wheeled wagon drawn by two or four horses with the passenger entrance in the rear. Within the next two years, five other lines began in different sections of the city, all terminating at the foot of Broadway. The fare was 16 trips for $1.

Fells Point also had the first horse drawn street car line. In July 1859 a series of trial trips with the horse cars were run with passengers riding free. Many citizens and merchants were wary of the contraptions—cars, pulled by horses, running on rails laid in the center of the streets. People worried that the horses wouldn't be able to drag the cars up steep hills, and would probably be crushed when they would lose control going down. Others claimed that lightning would strike the rails and the streets would be bombarded by electric bolts.

None of these supposed calamities occurred of course and the day after the first official run of a horse drawn street car, July 26, 1859, a newspaper reported:

> "Yesterday morning at 8 o'clock the passenger car, drawn by four horses, Mr. Charles Hancock, conductor, started at the foot of Broadway and ran to the intersection of Baltimore and North Streets. During the day the trip was repeated several times. The car was crowded on every trip. Owing to the amount of dirt on that part of the street newly paved, the car was several times thrown from the track on Baltimore Street, west of Central Avenue. No difficulty, however, was experienced in replacing the car on the track when thrown off, as the wheels took the rail again within a few feet. The motion of the car is very easy, and where the track was clear it moved rapidly."

The first line originated at North Street (Guilford Avenue) and Baltimore Street and ran over to Thames, east of Broadway. The fare at first was two cents but was soon raised to a nickel. The car barn was at 1724-26 Thames. At the end of each trip, the horse would pull the car into the barn, be unhitched and taken up a ramp to the second floor where he would be watered, rubbed down and fed. In the meantime, the car was pushed to the north end of the barn, a fresh horse was brought down the ramp and made ready for the return trip.

The first successful and largest bichromate factory in the United States was built in Fells Point. The plant was started in 1845 by Isaac Tyson, Jr., son of Jesse Tyson, a Baltimore grain merchant. Isaac was so interested in chemistry that he left a job in his father's grain warehouse to sign as apprentice to an apothecary. One day in 1813, while walking around the grounds of his family's summer home near Bare Hills, he noticed the gardener digging up heavy black rocks. The old man, who had once worked in a chemical plant in England making chrome pigments, told Isaac that the rocks were chromate. These, he said, are what we used to make chrome yellow out of in the old country.

Realizing the value of the ore, the young Tyson began mining it and exporting the raw material to England and Scotland. Shortly thereafter he found rich deposits in Jarrettsville and Rising Sun and by 1833 he held a monopoly on chrome mining in the United States. In 1828 he established a factory on what is now Washington Boulevard, for the manufacture of chrome yellow, but was unsuccessful. He tried again in 1833 and again failed.

Between 1828 and 1850 he supplied most of the chrome ore consumed in the world. He had cornered practically all known sources and had more raw material on hand than the European market could conveniently consume. To take care of this surplus, Tyson in 1845, erected a plant of his own at Block and Point Streets. It was the first plant in the United States in this field and its product for many years was bichromate of potash.

Isaac Tyson, Jr., headed the company until his death in 1861. It was taken over by his sons who operated it successfully. In the late 1860's the name of the firm was changed from Jesse Tyson & Company to the Baltimore Chrome Works. In 1905 the plant was acquired by the Mutual Chemical Company and in 1951 it was purchased by the Allied Chemical Corporation. It was modernized in 1952 and still runs at capacity.

With the discovery of gold in California in 1848 and in Australia in 1851 and because of increased trade with the Orient, there was a great demand for the new fast American Clipper ship. Because of their international reputation and abundance of labor, the Fells Point shipbuilders were swamped with orders. Between 1850 and 1859, 14 out of 27 Clipper ships constructed in Maryland were built in Fells Point, including the six largest.

Vessel	Tonnage	Built	Shipyard
Floral Temple	1,916	1853	J. J. Abrahams
Napier	1,811	1854	W. & G. Gardner
Whistling Wind	1,800	1855	W. & G. Gardner
Cherubim	1,796	1855	J. J. Abrahams
Carrier Dove	1,694	1855	J. J. Abrahams
Kate Hooper	1,489	1853	Hunt & Wagner

These ships were well built with beautiful lines. Most had short, exciting and sometimes disastrous careers.

The *Flora Temple,* the largest built in Maryland, had a tragic ending. On October 9, 1859 she left Macao for Havana with coolies. Six days later she struck an unknown reef in the China Sea and floundered. Eighteen crew members and 850 coolies were drowned.

The *Cherubim* was built for a group of Richmond, Virginia merchants. Her early days were spent sailing between the west coast of South America and England. On September 5, 1856 she ran down and sank the emigrant ship *Ocean Home,* resulting in heavy casualties. During a voyage in 1859 from New York to San Francisco a crew member as a prank poured salt into 40,000 gallons of drinking water, practically the entire supply. For the next 40 days the crew was allowed one pint per day per man. As she was owned by southern sympathizers the *Cherubim* spent the first three years of the Civil War lying idle at a dock in London. In 1863 she was sold to British interests and renamed *Lochee.*

Mary Whitridge

This ship, launched from Fells Point, holds the record as being
the fastest vessel to sail out of Baltimore

—*Merchants Club of Baltimore*

On October 5, 1855 the *Carrier Dove* left New York on her maiden voyage to San Francisco under the command of Captain Conner. Eight days later in a hurricane she lost her mainmast, fore and mizzen topmast with everything attached. On November 9 she finally limped into Rio de Janeiro, a wreck above the deck. The damage was so extensive, it was 60 days before she could continue her voyage to San Francisco. She had the reputation of being a "fast sailer." On October 23, 1856 she arrived in Valparaiso, Chile, 32 days from Melbourne, one day short of the record. An advertisement in the *New York Herald* claimed that in 1858 she went from Liverpool to Melbourne in 73 days and around the world in ten months. On March 3, 1876, while on a voyage from Liverpool to Philadelphia, she ran ashore and was abandoned.

The *Kate Hooper* spent the first five years sailing between New York, San Francisco and the Orient. In late October 1857 she left China with 600 coolies bound for Havana. After a week at sea the coolies mutinied and set fire to the ship. Order was restored after the ship officers shot four mutineers and hung the ringleader from the yardarm. On December 29, 1862, while lying in Hobson's Bay outside Melbourne, fire was discovered in one of the holds. In an attempt to save the ship and cargo, she was scuttled in 18 feet of water. This proved ineffective and she burned to the water's edge. It is alleged the fire was set by a Chinese member of the crew. The vessel was sold "as is" to a salvage company.

In 1855, a ship launched in Fells Point was to bear the reputation of being the fastest vessel to sail out of that harbor. The *Mary Whitridge* was built by Hunt & Wagner, on Fells Street south of Thames, for Thomas Whitridge, a Baltimore merchant. She was a 978 ton full-rigged ship, a new type which combined the stowage capacity of the old packet and the beauty and speed of the extreme Clipper ship. In the summer of 1855, under the command of Captain Cheeseborough, she left Baltimore for a voyage to England which would turn out to be one of the fastest passages in the history of sail. On board were a group of Baltimoreans, friends of Mr. Whitridge. On Sunday evening June 24, she left Cape Henry and reached the English Channel in 12 days and seven hours, having sailed 2,962 miles. This record has never been equalled by any sailing vessel.

On August 4, 1855 the *American and Commercial Advertiser* published this letter from a passenger:

> "I doubt much whether any sailing vessel ever crossed the Atlantic in less time. This abundantly proves the admirable qualities of the noble ship and skill, seamanship, and fidelity of Captain Cheeseborough who tested thoroughly her merits. I am sure few parties have ever such favorable conditions— a swift, staunch ship, a skillful captain, delightful weather, a quick passage, a good tempered company—all combined to make the voyage long to be remembered."

For the next 30 years the *Mary Whitridge* rarely returned to her home port. She was never without a cargo, sailing to all parts of the globe including two trips around Cape Horn to San Francisco. She was rebuilt in 1866 and immediately entered the China trade. She became one of the best Clipper ships in this trade, sailing mostly from the China ports of Shanghai and Foochow.

It was with some justice that the *New Orleans Commercial Bulletin* said that the Fells Point shipyards in Baltimore turned out the "finest vessels in the world."

Priscilla
Coffee vessel sailing from Fells Point between 1850 and 1900

In the late 1850's Fells Point shipbuilding again suffered a sharp decline. The Clipper ship era was nearing an end, steam was beginning to replace sail, and with the gold rush over, Clippers had a hard time finding cargoes.

The Association of Maryland Pilots was organized in Fells Point in 1852, with offices at 83 Thames Street, near Broadway. The pilots felt more could be accomplished by organized and coordinated activity. At one time the initiation fee was $1,000 for which a pilot received an undivided non-transferable share in the property of the association. Membership is attained after a four-year apprenticeship and passing a stiff examination. Once a member, each man takes his turn piloting a vessel to the Capes where he is picked up by the pilot boat and waits his turn to bring up an inbound vessel. All fees are collected by the association and once a month, after paying all expenses of the association, including the costs of manning, victualling and maintaining the pilot boats, the remainder is divided among the pilots.

It was different for the Bay pilots in the early 1800's. They had to collect their own fees and supply their own boats, manned by at least two licensed partners and one apprentice. At times there were as many as eight pilot boats cruising outside the Capes awaiting vessels bound for Fells Point. When a sail was sighted on the horizon all would race to reach the inbound vessel. The winning boat would throw a line to the ship and the pilot would be put aboard to bring the ship up the Bay. Life aboard the early pilot boats was hazardous; in the winter there were gales and ice to fight, in summer the threat of hurricanes. In bad weather it might be impossible for the pilot to transfer from the outbound vessel to the pilot boat. That meant the pilot was forced to continue on the vessel until the first port of call, returning to Baltimore by the next incoming vessel. According to one story a pilot was on a vessel for 72 days before returning home. Many of the early pilots lived in Fells Point, Benjamin Curtis on Apple Alley; Robert Berry and Humphrey Keeble on Wolf Street; William Halfpenny, on Aliceanna Street, and Will Pitt on Philpot Street.

It was through the pride of shipowners, masterful commanders and vigorous seamen, that a purely Baltimore and Fells Point enterprise was built in the 1850's. This was the Brazilian Coffee Fleet.

The opening of the commercial markets with Brazil began before the Civil War but the trade did not reach its peak until after the seas were clear of Confederate privateers. The *Empress Theresa* of Bandell's fleet was one of several Baltimore Clippers to pay tribute to Confederate privateers. She was captured November 1, 1864, by the *Olustee*. Captain Nathaniel Collin Walker was in command of this ship bound from Rio to Baltimore, Mrs. Walker, with a baby in arms, her sister, Captain Walker and the crew were invited to come aboard the *Olustee* and remain while they witnessed the burning of the *Empress Theresa*. The prisoners were well treated and later transferred to a schooner and landed in New York. Alfred H. Walker, who served for many years as deputy warden of the Maryland Penitentiary, was that babe in arms.

Between 1840 and 1900, three ships, 48 barks, 11 barkentines, 11 brigs and two schooners were engaged in the coffee trade. Even with this number, many of which flew the house flag of a Baltimore merchant, other bottoms had to be chartered to meet the demand for outward and inward cargo.

The coffee trade was the natural counterpart of the flour trade and constitutes a significant chapter in the history of the port of Baltimore. Competition between the ports of Baltimore and New York was especially keen from 1835 to 1900. Since New

Josephine
One of the most successful vessels in the Baltimore coffee fleet

York's western flour was not successful in tropical climates, ships leaving that port had difficulty in getting cargoes for the trip south. Baltimore, offering flour from the mills of Hazall in Richmond, and products from Gambrill's in Ellicott City and Ilchester assured the Clippers sailing out of the port a full cargo.

During this time most of the coffee fleet loaded and discharged its cargoes at Fells Point. Bags of coffee were unloaded on a platform by horse drawn ropes attached to the windlass on the ship. From the platform the bags were carried on the backs of the laborers to the beam scales. After weighing the coffee was moved by hand wagons to the warehouse. If the bags were to be stored above the first floor they were placed in a rope or canvas sling and hoisted by placing a block and fall on an iron hook over the top floor door. The rope fall was pulled by a team of horses and the sling was then hoisted to the second, third or fourth floor. The two largest warehouses and wharves were Brown's Wharf at the foot of Broadway and Belt's Wharf at the foot of Fells Street.

The Pendergast, Rollins, Whitridge and Jenkins fleets discharged their cargoes from South America at Brown's Wharf. Belt's Wharf was the terminal of the fleet of the Baltimore merchant C. Morton Stewart. He had preferred the barkentine-type vessel, while Mr. Rollins and others held to the Baltimore-built bark model. The Baltimore vessels were built at Fells Point exclusively for this trade which gave them a reputation of being the cleanest and daintiest merchant craft afloat. The decks, crews' and officers' quarters were always sandstoned before entering a port. Every morning the floors in all quarters were scrubbed with lime water, which kept them clean and deodorized. Not all of these splendid ships were blessed with good luck.

The first *Josephine* was built at Belfast, Maine in 1892 for C. Morton Stewart. On May 16, 1895, while bound from Rio de Janeiro with 9,000 bags of coffee consigned to Baltimore, she ran aground at night in thick fog at Little Island, south of Virginia Beach, Virginia. Life-saving crews from the nearby beach went to her aid and rescued some of the crew. A few men remained aboard with hope of refloating the vessel. A salvage company removed some of the cargo, but bad weather forced them to cancel their operations. After being pounded by heavy seas, the *Josephine* finally capsized and was declared a total wreck.

Mr. Stewart had the second *Josephine* built in 1896 which was the most successful vessel in the Baltimore Coffee Fleet. This sleek barkentine held the record for making the fastest passage from Rio de Janeiro to Baltimore. In May, 1903, she was reported off Cape Henry taking pilot on board in 22 days from the Sugar Loaf. This was such amazing time that both her owner and the marine solons of the Fells Point waterfront doubted the report. She continued in the coffee trade until after the turn of the century. Later she was sent to Philadelphia to be rigged as a four-masted schooner. On April 30, 1922, while bound from Jacksonville to Philadelphia with a cargo of lumber, she was found by the Coast Guard cutter *Seminole* abandoned at sea. She was towed to Southport, North Carolina and beached as a derelict.

The list of coffee ships sailing out of Fells Point discloses many attractive names: *Adelaide, Virginia Dare, Priscilla, Caroline, Justina* and *Henrietta*. Masculine names were regarded as out of harmony with the worldwide gender of "she" as applied to ships. Men of the sea believe there never has been anything more beautiful and appropriate for a ship than a simple feminine name.

The captains of the coffee fleet were a breed of their own. They were hard sailors of the old school, frequently performing miracles of dead reckoning, driving their vessels through fair weather and foul, but not too conservative to accept innovations. An example was Captain Erickson of the *Frances*. Ashore he was a sedate, well-dressed business man, but once at sea he looked and acted like a pirate. In good weather he would read dime novels from his steamer chair near the wheel, clad in slippers and an old greasy cap, with his pants rolled up to his knees. At three o'clock, up would come the cockney cook with the Captain's "tea," a half pint of coffee and a huge doughnut. The captain would take his cup, spit out his chew of tobacco on the tray and tell the cook to "get the hell off the poopdeck." Sometimes he would make a little money on the side by smuggling diamonds and ostrich feathers out of Brazil, a practice frequently indulged in by the old skippers.

On one of his trips to Rio from Fells Point, Captain William Forbes, commanding the *Albemarle* of the Whedbee Dickinson fleet, arrived during a revolution. The coffee fleet lay at anchor outside the harbor because the new government had closed the port. The harbor was heavily guarded at its entrance by the guns of the fort. Captain Forbes decided that staying at anchor was a loss of time. Disregarding the fort's signals that he would be fired on if he tried to enter, he hoisted sails and started into the port. The Brazilian officers were evidently too surprised to give the order to open fire as the *Albemarle* swept past in a cloud of canvas. A more accurate reason, probably, was that the new government did not wish to start any trouble with the United States. The *Albemarle* returned with the first cargo of the year and her exploit was discussed for days along the waterfront. As late as 1922, a few of the old coffee fleet captains, such as Peter Eriksson and Edward Laplanche, were still following their profession on the bridges of steamers.

After the turn of the century, Baltimore became second to New York as the chief port of coffee importation, the latter offering a better distribution of the product. With the increased use of steam, the Baltimore coffee fleet was doomed.

Because many ships had been lost at sea, abandoned or converted to barges, only a few sailed out of the Chesapeake Bay at the beginning of the 20th century. Some of the last ships to unload coffee in Fells Point were the *Gray Eagle, Gramaliel, Templar* and *Yamayden.*

The Changing Years

1860-1899

During the first three months of 1861, Baltimore was torn apart by the supporters of the North and South. The strained atmosphere on the Fells Point waterfront was further aggravated on April 14 by a riot when the bark *Fanny Crewshaw* flew a secession flag. On April 26, the factional tensions were so strong that George P. Kane, marshall of Baltimore, issued the following order:

> "I have represented to the Mayor and Board of Police that the peace of the city is likely to be disturbed by the display of various flags, in different parts of the city, in hands of parties disposed to disorder and riot. I do hereby, by their instructions, order that no flag be raised in any place or carried through the streets, during the session of the legislature now meeting in Frederick. This order will be strictly enforced, without respect to persons, and I feel convinced that all good citizens will concur in its propriety."

The citizens of Fells Point, demonstrating their affection for their country, refused to lower the American flag. It was not until Marshall Kane dispatched a squad of policemen to the Point that the flag was taken down. The repercussions from the Baltimore riots would have a deadly effect on the Fells Point shipyards and wharves.

The northern section of the country began to assail Baltimore through the press. An editorial in the *New York Tribune* read:

> "One section of the country is only semi-civilized in a society so constituted it is not strange that there should be found many persons who could conceive and execute some diabolical plot of slaughter."

In Boston, incensed by the attack on the Sixth Massachusetts Infantry, the natives began to sing:

> "There's swelling cry for vengeance on the counterfeits of men who haunt that hold of pirates—that foul assassin's den!"

The Mayor of Baltimore, fearing more bloodshed, destroyed the bridges of the Northern Central and the Philadelphia, Wilmington and Baltimore railroads, north of the city, thus cutting off Baltimore and Fells Point. The Baltimore and Ohio railroad, which served the port from the west, was immobilized by the raids of the Confederate calvary. When the Fells Point links with the north and west were broken, trade came to a halt.

Somerset

One of the first merchant ships to fly the American
flag on the Atlantic Ocean after the Civil War

—Peale Museum

The Confederacy knew that Baltimore, along with Fells Point with its warehouses and wharves, was a natural depot for the federal armies in Virginia. The South was so anxious to win Maryland over to its side that it favored the Baltimore ships when captured by Confederate privateers. Out of the hundreds of ships seized or destroyed by the raiders, only ten had cleared from or were bound to Baltimore.

Charles W. Read of Mississippi was a second lieutenant on the Confederate privateer *Florida* under the command of Captain Maffitt. On May 6, 1863 the *Florida* captured the *Clarence* bound for Brown's Wharf in Fells Point with a full cargo of Brazilian coffee. A few hours after the capture, Lt. Read presented the following letter to Captain Maffitt:

"Sir: I propose to take the brig which we have just captured, and with a crew of 20 men to proceed to Hampton Roads and cut out a gunboat or steamer of the enemy. As I would be in possession of the Brig's papers, and as the crew would be not large enough to excite suspicion, there can be no doubt of my passing Fortress Monroe successfully. Once in the Roads I would prepare to avail my self of any circumstances which might present for gaining the check of an enemy's vessel. If it was found impossible to board a gunboat or merchant steamers, it would be possible to fire the shipping at Baltimore."

Very respectfully, your obedient servant
C. W. Read
Second Lieutenant, C.S. Navy

Captain Maffitt was intrigued by the idea and had the *Clarence* outfitted for Lt. Read. After taking command, the young officer made the ship more formidable, in appearance at least, by adding several wooden guns. The *Clarence* captured a number of federal merchant ships as it made its way north to the Chesapeake Bay. From a northern newspaper found aboard one of his prizes, Lt. Read learned that the security at Hampton Roads was so strict that only a Union transport carrying government goods could get through. He decided to cruise along the coast to try to capture a transport and "in the meantime do all possible damage to the enemy commerce." When Read was captured on June 24, after he had destroyed 21 Union merchant ships, his plan for burning the shipping in Baltimore was still only a dream.

During the first three years of the war Fells Point suffered immeasurably. The military authorities enforced an embargo which almost eliminated the coffee and flour trade. Wharves and warehouses were barren and shipyards lay idle. The merchants of Fells Point were forced to import or export their goods through one of the northern ports. In the fall of 1863 conditions improved slightly as several Union expeditions were outfitted for operations against the South. Some shipyards were re-activated when a number of U. S. naval vessels were sent to the Point for repairs and refitting. Hostilities ended on April 9, 1865, but the Civil War had rendered the blow which ended Fells Point's status as a major shipbuilding center.

That same year one of the most successful non-shipping enterprises in Fells Point began. J. J. Lacy, Inc., manufacturers of iron castings, opened its doors at 1401 Block Street. The business is still operated today at the original location by the Lacy family.

In the spring of 1865 two prominent Baltimoreans, John W. Garrett, president of the B & O Railroad, and George S. Brown, president of Alex. Brown & Sons,

East End of Thames Street, 1869

Baltimore's leading banking institution, were determined to try and recapture the commerce that Baltimore had enjoyed before the war.

Mr. Garrett was convinced the port needed a transatlantic steamship line. With the approval of his company he purchased three wooden screw ships from the U. S. government which had been used as blockaders during the war. After repairs and alterations, they were named the *Worcester, Carroll* and *Somerset.* They were small brig-rigged and had limited passenger accommodations. The *Worcester,* the largest, was 218 feet long, 1,500 gross tons and had a speed of ten knots.

Fells Point was buzzing with excitement as the day of the inauguration of the line approached. On Friday, September 29, 1865 this report appeared in the *Baltimore Sun:*

"The steamship, *Somerset,* one of the vessels about to be inaugurated between this port and Liverpool, and which has been undergoing extensive repairs and alterations, is now so far completed as to be able to start on her first trip across the ocean, as the pioneer of the enterprise, the success of which is of such importance to the mercantile interest of Baltimore. In addition to the elaborate work put upon the hull of the vessel, Messrs. Jas. Clark & Co. of the People's Machine & Boiler Works, have placed a new shaft in her and her engines have been thoroughly overhauled and refitted. A brief trial trip of the *Somerset* was made a few days since, when a number of gentlemen interested in the enterprise were on board, and after running some 16 miles expressed themselves perfectly satisfied with the ship in every respect. With 15 pounds of steam she made 35 revolutions per minute, and it was asserted that she can make ten knots with 25 pounds of steam, her usual standard. At noon tomorrow, the *Somerset* leaves this port for Liverpool. She will start from Henderson's Wharf, foot of Fell Street. All her cargo is aboard, several persons are booked as passengers. The cargo is nearly as follows: 300 bales of cotton, 100 hogsheads of tobacco, 6,000 bushels of corn, 800 sacks oil-cake, 40 tons bark, a large quantity of dye-stuffs, canned fruits and miscellaneous articles. During yesterday about 50 shipjoiners and painters were at work in her, and with this force, by Saturday the repairs and alterations will be completed.

"At and around Henderson's wharf there will be ample room for many persons to congregate at the time of the departure of the vessel, the occasion being one of which Baltimoreans may be truly proud. As the ship leaves the wharf she will be saluted from Fort Federal Hill and by the U.S. revenue cutter, and will also be saluted as she passes Fort McHenry. These salutes will be returned by the *Somerset.* The U.S. revenue cutter will convey a large party of ladies and gentlemen some distance down the bay. Among these will be Major Gen. Hancock, Hon. Thomas Swann, Governor-elect, Mayor Chapman, John W. Garrett, Esq., and other distinguished gentlemen. It is understood that a steamboat will leave the adjoining wharf, and accompany the *Somerset* as far as North Point, on board of which persons can take a short excursion and witness the departure of the pioneer ship of this ocean line between Baltimore and Liverpool."

The next morning thousands of spectators along the shores of Fells Point

Northern Central Railroad Elevator
Built at Thames and Caroline Streets in 1871

cheered as the *Somerset* left on her maiden voyage. The three ships were the first merchant vessels to fly the American flag on the Atlantic Ocean after the Civil War. The operation lasted only three years because it could not compete with the new iron ships of the North German Lloyd line. Nevertheless, the three small steamers opened a new era for the port of Baltimore.

On October 30, 1865, Mr. Brown organized a company to establish a coast-wide steamship line from Baltimore to Charleston and Havana. Capital was quickly acquired and a fleet of steamers was built. In December, the first vessel sailed from Brown's Wharf with a full cargo. The company was so successful that in three years New Orleans was added to the route. The small line was responsible for the port of Baltimore re-opening its trade with the South.

Due to the foresight of such men as George S. Brown and John W. Garrett, Baltimore was regaining its position as a world port.

During the latter part of the 1860's a large number of German immigrants arrived and settled in Fells Point, many of whom would become prominent Baltimoreans. The sailing vessels carrying the immigrants berthed at Corner's Wharf, on Thames Street between Broadway and Ann.

An unusual story about Corner's Wharf has been told by Charles A. Thalheimer, former deputy collector of the port. His father landed there as a German immigrant after having made the voyage across the Atlantic on a sailing vessel. His mother, also a native of Germany, arrived at the same wharf a few years later. When Mr. Thalheimer entered the customs service as a young man he was assigned to the duties of a clerk on Corner's Wharf, the same terminal on which his father and mother first touched American soil.

County Wharf was once the scene of a colorful tradition. When a German brewmaster would sail for a vacation in the homeland, a major part of the German quarter would turn out to bid farewell. A beer wagon would be sent to the wharf and by the time the brewmaster and his family arrived in their coach, the party and folk singing were well under way.

Although John W. Garrett was instrumental in revitalizing Fells Point after the Civil War, he signed an agreement on January 21, 1867 which began a chain of events from which Fells Point never recovered. The agreement between the Baltimore and Ohio and the North German Lloyd Steamship line was to run at least two new large iron steamers between Baltimore and Bremen. The wharves in Fells Point were too small to accommodate the new steamers so Garrett decided to develop Locust Point directly across the Patapsco River from the Point into a modern deep-water terminal. Large piers with rail sidings, grain elevators, coal bins and supporting warehouses were constructed. The terminal worked so well that a few years later the Pennsylvania Railroad decided to duplicate it in Canton. In 1870 the only deep water commerce left in Fells Point was the coffee and flour trade.

During this period the Northern Central Railroad (successor to the P W & B Railroad) began to lay tracks from the President Street yards to the warehouses in Fells Point. In 1871 the railroad built a small grain elevator at Caroline and Thames Streets. The next year the Jackson Wharf Freight Station (Thames Street between Caroline and Bond Streets) and three small finger piers were constructed. For the next 50 years, one or more sailing vessels were loading or discharging cargo— barks loading flour for South America and the small bay schooners unloading water-

Jackson's Wharf

—*Baltimore Sunpapers*

melons and green tomatoes. Captain Leonard S. Tawes in his book, *Coasting Captain,* mentions loading his schooner *City of Baltimore* at Jacksons Wharf with bags of flour for the West Indies. Wagon loads of canned goods from nearby packing houses were handled daily at the freight station. Special trains carrying oysters were shipped from Jacksons Wharf, and each car carried a banner, "Maryland Oysters."

Due to a city ordinance prohibiting the use of steam locomotives on streets, the shifting of cars from the railroad yards to sidings was handled by a team of eight Percherons. One team could pull two or three cars. If the load were particularly heavy, two or even three teams would be hitched in tandem. When the ordinance was rescinded in 1917, the railroad replaced the horses with an electric tractor.

Between 1870 and 1880 a few Fells Point shipyards continued to build small barks and schooners for trade on the Chesapeake Bay, and skipjacks for oyster dredging. The workmanship in the yards was of the highest quality. The schooner *Kate Darlington,* for example, built in 1889 by H. Brusstar & Brother, Philpot and Point Streets, was still freighting lumber from the western shore of Virginia to the Fells Point lumber yards after 50 years. When other shipyards were forced to close, their property was quickly acquired by lumber, canning and packing companies. Some of the early canners and packers at the Point were W. Fletcher Penz, W. L. Ellis & Co., W. W. Bower and E. B. Mallory & Co.

In 1882 the Baltimore Cotton Compress Company (an Alex. Brown & Sons enterprise) constructed a cotton compress in Fells Point at the foot of Bond Street. The large uncompressed bales were brought to Baltimore by steamboats of the Merchants and Miners Transportation Co., the Old Bay Line and several small lines. The cotton, after being compressed, was weighed and graded. The bales were then exported or stored in Brown's Wharf Warehouse, adjacent to the cotton compress. For the next ten years the compress worked at capacity until destroyed by fire on December 13, 1892. Firemen battled the blaze for two days and the fireboat *Cataract* was on the scene for seven days spraying down the smoldering cotton.

The *Cataract,* the first fireboat in Baltimore, was built in Fells Point by the E. J. Codd Company, 700 South Caroline Street, at Brusstar's shipyard, Philpot and Point Streets, at a cost of $17,425.25. Her hull and beams were wood and she was equipped with piston pumps with a capacity of 4,400 gallons per minute. On July 1, 1891, she was assigned to the new Engine Co., No. 16, on Commercial Wharf, near the foot of Broadway. Captain Richard A. Lindsay was commander.

In the middle 1870's a group of Polish immigrants settled in Fells Point. The majority of the men worked as stevedores and most of the women had seasonal jobs in the local canning factories. Because most were staunch Catholics their main concern was to found a parish and build a church. About 1877 they formed the St. Stanislaus Society to collect funds to finance the construction. The next step was to procure the services of a priest, scarce in those days in America. The Rev. Peter Koncz of Wilno, Poland, was invited to take charge of the new parish and accepted the invitation. The first church was a rented house on the southwest corner of Fleet and Bond Streets. In 1880, under the supervision of Father Koncz, a church, with school facilities, was built on the southwest corner of Ann and Aliceanna Streets. Father Koncz, conversant also in Lithuanian, did extensive missionary work among the immigrants. He died on February 8, 1886. His death was said to have resulted from a beating by unknown assailants.

Horses shifting cars

Because a city ordinance prohibited the use of steam locomotives on the streets, the
shifting of cars from the railroad yards to the sidings was handled
by a team of eight Percherons

—Baltimore Sunpapers

In 1881, through the preaching of Dwight L. Moody in Baltimore, the Port Mission was started in Fells Point to conduct gospel work among the seamen. It was organized by a group of prominent Baltimoreans, among them Gustavas Ober, J. Levering, L. M. Levering, B. W. Jenkins and W. Dugdale. The first services were held in a small house on Shakespeare Street and the following year the mission's quarters were moved to 800 South Broadway. In 1884 it was forced to seek larger quarters at 815 South Broadway and in 1895 it was enlarged by acquiring the four-story building at 813 South Broadway. In the early days many needy seamen were provided with meals and lodging. The files of the mission are filled with letters written by seamen from all over the world praising the work it was accomplishing in Baltimore. The seamen's activities are an important branch of the mission work, but its greatest service has been among the families throughout the city.

A remarkable instance involving the Mission is the case of Feodor Jakimik. In 1894 he picked up a religious pamphlet at a meeting and put it in his pocket. Several days later he packed the suit in his trunk, the unread pamphlet still in the pocket. A year passed, he came upon the pamphlet and after reading its message, he was so impressed with it that he left Baltimore to preach that gospel to his people in Russia.

The Port Mission, still at 813-15 South Broadway, is not a church, though it encourages its members to join a church of their choice. The mission is inter-denominational and is sustained by voluntary offerings. Another similar establishment was the Anchorage. It was organized on April 27, 1892 at a meeting of the Port Mission's Women's Auxiliary. The purpose was "to maintain under Christian influences a boarding house for seamen, a home-away-from-home, a social and recreational center where the seafarer might find safe refuge while in port."

At that time seamen could secure lodgings only at the "crimps"—rooming houses connected with saloons, brothels and gambling establishments where they were quickly separated from their hard-earned wages.

The Anchorage began its work in rented quarters at 1737 Thames Street now the site of the Recreation Pier. Repairs and alterations were necessary, thus delaying the opening until July 7, 1892. The number of seamen who made this their home when in port demonstrated the need for such an establishment and within a few years it was necessary to secure larger quarters.

In 1900 the central unit of the present property at Broadway and Thames Street was erected and opened on December 3. Originally a boarding house, the Anchorage grew to be a home and spiritual, social and service center for thousands of merchant seamen. During 1908 it became a separate organization, The Anchorage of Baltimore City.

The adjoining building at 1644 Thames Street was purchased in 1920 and in 1925 the addition, fronting on Broadway, was built. The combined property had 106 rooms accommodating 165 seamen. Its facilities included a reading and writing room, lobby, assembly room, baggage room and restaurant. The responsibility had become so great and the activities so numerous that the Board of Managers decided in 1929 to place the work in the hands of a larger Christian organization experienced in working with men. The board invited the Y M C A to take over the Anchorage and it did so in July 1, 1929.

In 1955, citing financial reasons, the Community Chest cut off the Anchorage as a branch of the Y M C A. The hotel was forced to close that year after serving seamen for almost half a century. This landmark still stands in Fells Point; it is now used to store vinegar.

Fells Point also made history in areas other than in the shipping industry. One innovative thinker it claims as a native son was Isadore Noah, the father of many modern business tactics. Noah, born in 1860 at 60 South Broadway, owned a store at Broadway and Eastern, B. Noah and Son. In 1889 he replaced the store with what would become the first up-to-date department store on the Point. He was a maverick in many ways: he was the first to use an arc light to illuminate the outside of his store; he was the first to subscribe to streetcar advertising; to have attractive window displays; to run a full page ad in a Baltimore paper and the first to use photo-engraving in his ads. He also, according to some reports, was the one who invented the bargain sale. He retired from the business in 1898 while still a young man.

Two major ice houses were located in Fells Point: the American Ice Company, on Wolfe Street between Thames and Fells Streets and the Maine Lake Ice Company, at the foot of Block Street. Ice was cut during the winter on the Kennebec and other fresh water Maine rivers and stored in ice houses on the river banks. A large fleet of two- and three-masted schooners carried coal from Baltimore to the Northern ports and returned with cargoes of ice. The blocks of ice were unloaded by the vessels' donkey engines by chute into the icehouse. There they were stored layer by layer and hoisted to the upper levels by tongs, ropes and pulleys. Straw and sawdust were placed between each layer of ice for insulation.

With the approach of the 20th century only a few shipyards were left in Fells Point, and these were being used for dry docking and as repair yards for small bay sailing vessels.

The Declining Years

1900-1964

Fells Point continued to grow industrially as it moved into the 1900's. New canning and packing plants were constructed in its eastern section. D. E. Foote, Lord Mott, William Taylor & Son and W. H. Roberts plants were in the 2000 block of Aliceanna Street, while Thomas Moore and J. C. Farren established their businesses at the foot of Wolfe Street.

Over the years, the canning and packing industry had changed from a seasonal to a year-round operation. Oysters from the Chesapeake Bay were packed in the winter months, pineapples from the Bahama Islands from spring to July and tomatoes from nearby counties and the Eastern Shore in the summer and fall. The docks at the canneries were filled with all types of sailing craft: bugeyes and sloops loaded to the decks with oysters freshly dredged from the bay, and schooners which had returned from the Eleuthera and Cat Islands in the Bahamas with fresh pineapples. The fruit had been loaded while still green and allowed to ripen during the trip to Fells Point. In late July the same schooners would start freighting the popular Eastern Shore tomato to the canneries. The labor supply was more than ample as entire families were employed.

As the demand for storage of the finished products increased, a modern warehouse was built at the foot of Bond Street by the Terminal Warehouse Company. Other new industries included the fertilizer plants of Isaac Robinson & Company and L. Sonneborn & Sons Chemical Company on Philpot Street, and the Lauer & Suter Candy Company on Block Street.

Shortly after the turn of the century—four years and 38 days to be exact—Fells Point was saved from a possible disaster by the *William Windom,* a small United States revenue cutter.

Built in 1896 at Dubuque, Iowa for the federal government she was steel hulled 170 feet long, with a 27 foot beam, nine foot draft and a gross tonnage of 398 tons. After being commissioned she was sent to Baltimore as a revenue cutter. Her commander was Captain George E. McConnell and her crew consisted of five commissioned officers and ten seamen. Her home berth was Chases's Wharf at Philpot and Thames Streets, the western end of Fells Point.

On Saturday, February 6, 1904, the *Windom* left Baltimore for a routine trip to Annapolis. Captain McConnell received a message at noon on Sunday of a serious fire in Baltimore. He was told to proceed there immediately. Early Sunday

Samuel H. Tagart
Broadway-Locust Point Ferry, 1902

—Peale Museum

William Windom
A small U. S. revenue cutter that saved Fells Point from a near disaster

—*Author's Collection*

evening, the fire, gathering momentum from the 30 mph winds, blazed south toward the five long piers stretching off Pratt Street. Upon arriving in Baltimore the *Windom* was sent to this area to fight the fire on the docks and to assist in moving to safe anchorage the barges berthed at those piers. All night long the *Windom* fought a losing battle, the docks on Pratt Street were gutted.

By midnight, with the fire spreading eastward, Fells Point panicked. Children, parents and old folks were in tears as people started piling their household goods on the sidewalks. Merchants at the foot of Broadway began removing their goods and stowing them in the street until they could be carted away. Horses and wagons were in great demand, and teamsters raised their prices hourly. Men, women and children, carrying whatever they could, rushed to the Broadway ferry to cross to Locust Point. Due to the uncontrollable crowds trying to board the ferry, the authorities were forced to turn most of them away. Many residents of the Point went to St. Stanislaus Catholic Church, at Ann and Aliceanna Streets, to pray for deliverance from the flames.

The firemen's strategy was to keep the fire on the west side of Jones Falls, but between 11 a.m. and 1 p.m. Monday, the flames jumped over to the east side. The fire began spreading along the waterfront towards Fells Point. The main worry of the authorities was the Shryock Lumber Company on Philpot Street near Thames. This yard contained a barn with over 5,000,000 feet of lumber and if ignited, Fells Point was doomed. The *Windom* was ordered off-shore of Shryock's yard to pour all the water it could pump on the lumber stored there. Even though the officers and crew of the *Windom* were exhausted—they had been on duty for over 36 hours— they knew the fire had to be stopped at this point. Every available hose aboard the vessel was used as the flames roared down Philpot Street. The fertilizer works of Isaac Robinson & Company and L. Sonneborn & Sons Chemical Company went up. Then the Maine Lake Ice Company was engulfed and the fire moved closer to the Shryock's lumber yard. But with the combined force of the water poured on the lumber by the crew of the *Windom,* aided by the wind which had shifted to the north, the fire was checked. Fells Point was saved. A short time later, the merchants of Fells Point, headed by Mr. Shryock, held a reception for the men of the *William Windom.* Captain McConnell and his crew were commended and each man was presented with a gold piece and a bottle of champagne. The *Windom* continued to serve as revenue cutter until she was decommissioned in the early part of 1930. On November 13, 1930 she was sold to the Weiss Motor Lines for $4,501 and was dismantled and converted to a bay barge.

That Sunday, February 7, as the fire was spreading towards Fells Point, Walter Gibowicz and Catherine Goscinski were to be married at St. Stanislaus Church. Despite the near panic in the Point, Catherine had made up her mind that the wedding would take place. Everyone else in the neighborhood was moving personal belongings from their homes, but Eva Goscinski, Catherine's mother, removed only three items—a goose feather mattress and two pillows. She left the mattress in the vestibule of the church and sat through the wedding ceremony clutching a pillow under each arm. It is an old Polish custom to present a newly-wed couple with a goose feather mattress and pillows immediately after the ceremony and Mrs. Goscinski made sure the custom was carried out, regardless of the possibility of losing her own possessions.

In 1912 the city council authorized the building of a pier in Fells Point for

Cataract

The first fireboat in Baltimore, built in Fells Point, fighting the
great fire of 1904 as it neared the Point

—Peale Museum

Bell Tower

Old Shipbuilders Union bell tower, foot of Caroline Street
below Lancaster, 1908

the dual purpose of accommodating commercial ships and providing a recreational facility for the area citizens. The Recreation Pier, Thames Street between Broadway and Ann, was dedicated on August 20, 1914. It was built of tapestry brick and Indiana limestone at the cost of $1,000,000. The ballroom on the upper floor was one of the largest in the city and is noted for its fine plaster work and oak trim. It was one of the first municipal dance halls in the country.

When war was declared on April 6, 1917, the patriotic spirit which had been so apparent in Fells Point 100 years before still prevailed. The young men enlisted and other able-bodied men worked as stevedores loading military cargoes or as carpenters building stalls on vessels transporting horses to France. Older men, women and children were employed in the canning factories. These operated seven days a week, 24 hours a day.

After the war, the first cargo of German potash (a fertilizer ingredient) arriving in Baltimore was unloaded at Block Street Wharf & Warehouse Co., at the foot of Block Street. The bulk potash was unloaded by tubs and stockpiled in the warehouse until redelivered to local fertilizer plants by scows or loaded on schooners and rams for the plants on the Eastern Shore. For the next 17 years over one million tons were handled at this location.

One of the popular features during the summers of the early 1920's, was the excursion boat *Dreamland,* which sailed from the foot of Broadway. A sidewheeler about 300 foot long, she was the largest vessel of its kind in Baltimore. Each summer thousands of Baltimoreans rode the *Dreamland* down to Chesapeake Beach for a day of fun. Each night the steamer would sail on a moonlight cruise. The small house at 904 South Broadway, built just after the Civil War, was used as the ticket office. After laying idle for many years the building was purchased in 1970 by the Brown Wharf and Warehouse Company to be torn down to provide parking for their employees. After removing the roof and floors, the demolition was stopped because of protests from preservationists. It was sold in 1972 to a local enthusiast who planned to restore it.

Duke, a big dog of questionable ancestry who was loved by every child in the neighborhood, was another favorite regular on the Point. He was owned by Seal Holms, who operated a combination bar and boarding house in the vicinity of Thames and Fells Streets. Besides playing with children, Duke had a chore which he seemed to enjoy—shopping at the Broadway Market. Whenever Holms needed fresh provisions he would put his list and money in a market basket. Duke would pick the basket up by the handle and with his head held high, trot up Thames Street to a certain stall in the market. After the order was filled the dog would return home with the full basket. Everyone in Fells Point knew Duke as a gentle dog but they also knew he could be disagreeable if stopped during one of his shopping expeditions.

Fells Point celebrated its Bicentennial from September 7 to September 13, 1930. Sponsored by the Civic Club of East Baltimore, the week-long activities included a marathon race, parade and Mardi Gras party. The souvenir program, "Fells Point Bicentennial Jubilee," presented the early history of Fells Point in a light and interesting manner. Its foreword declared:

> "In a number of instances historians have given credit to the City of Baltimore as a whole for the happenings and historical developments taking place at Fells Point during the 200 years since its founding."

Dreamland docked at the Foot of Broadway, 1920's

Block Street Wharf and Warehouse in 1935

—Author's Collection

When the crash of 1929 and the ensuing Depression came, Fells Point did not suffer as badly as other communities. Two intercoastal steamship lines began operating; Lykes Line ships berthed at Henderson's Wharf, at the foot of Fell Street, and the Southern Pacific Steamship Lines terminal was Jackson's Wharf, Caroline and Thames Streets. During the early 30's Texas suffered a severe drought and as both lines served this area they were assured full cargoes south, especially of canned tomatoes. For the next five years the canneries of Fells Point ran at capacity. A large number of schooners and powerboats delivered loads of tomatoes from the Eastern Shore to each of the steamship lines.

During a seamen's strike, in the middle of the 1930's, an unreported shanghaing occurred in Fells Point. One winter afternoon the president of the terminal handling the Southern Pacific Lines called his son, who was working on another job for the company in Canton, and told him to bring four of his laborers to Jackson's Wharf. The S/S *El Estero* was ready to sail for Texas and as the crew was four men short, the Coast Guard refused to let the ship leave. The young man was advised to tell the laborers that they were to help shift the vessel from Jackson's Wharf to Sparrows Point. Piling the men in his Model A Ford, he drove them through the picket line at Jackson's Wharf and placed them aboard the *El Estero* which sailed for Texas that night. Thirty years later, the same man—older and wiser, attended a dance at a local country club. While checking his coat, he was greeted with, "Hello, Cap, its been 30 years since I have seen you." He was unable to speak as he recognized the man behind the counter as one of the four he had shanghaied years before. The tension was quickly broken as the man continued, "I want to thank you for putting me aboard the *El Estero* that day, because when I landed in Texas I was immediately hired as an able seaman on a tanker. After working at sea for 25 years for the same company, I am now retired with a fine pension." A true story. I ought to know, as I am the one who put that man aboard the *El Estero* many years ago.

The captain of the *El Iselo*, which docked regularly at Jackson's Wharf, was P. H. Perry. He was an accomplished artist and spent his leisure time in port painting scenes of Fells Point. Unfortunately, as far as anyone can ascertain, only three of his paintings exist.

The success of the intercoastal lines seemed to stimulate the marine interests in Fells Point. In 1935 Rukert Terminals replaced the old wharf at the foot of Caroline Street with a modern pier capable of docking two vessels. Terminal Warehouse, at the foot of Bond Street, lengthened its pier in 1937 to accommodate deep sea freighters.

Despite these improvements, though, Fells Point was slowly changing and deteriorating. In the middle 1930's many original Fells Point houses were razed for commercial enterprises. The most notable were the homes on the northwest corner of Block and Caroline Streets, which were torn down and replaced by a one-story warehouse. On February 10, 1937, one of the small finger piers at Jackson's Wharf freight station suddenly fell into the harbor, carrying two men and seven box cars with it. The two men were rescued by the crew of a tugboat docked nearby. The pier, which had been in service for over 65 years, was never replaced.

Just prior to World War II, another marine activity in Fells Point was terminated. Since the turn of the century, one or more schooners had always been unloading lumber at the yards on Lancaster or Philpot Streets. The lumber was usually shipped from the sawmills on the western shore of Virginia, but occasionally the

Houses being torn down
Many of the original homes were razed in the middle 1930's
for commercial purposes

—Author's Collection

Collapse of Jackson's Wharf

In February, 1937, one of the small finger piers at Jackson's Wharf freight station

fell into the harbor carrying two men and seven box cars with it.

The men were rescued. The 65 year old pier has not been replaced

—Baltimore News American

larger schooners would make a trip to Elizabeth, N. C. for a load of Georgia pine. With the improvement of highways, the lumber companies found it more economical to bring the lumber to Baltimore by truck for direct distribution.

The Southern Pacific and Lykes steamship lines continued to operate in Fells Point until the beginning of World War II, at which time the U. S. Maritime Commission took over the fleets of both lines and converted the vessels into military transports. The marine activity in Fells Point during the war was minimal, with one exception—the unloading of the last full-rigged Clipper ship carrying cargo into the port of Baltimore.

The *Hawaiian Isles* was built in 1892 at Glasgow, Scotland by D. Connell & Company, 260.9 feet long, 43.2 foot beam, 23.6 foot depth, 2,345 gross tons, for the Hawaiian Construction Co., Honolulu. After passing through several hands, she was purchased in 1910 from the Matson Navigation Company by the Alaska Packers Association and renamed *Star of Greenland*. After serving 20 years with this company, she passed into Swedish hands and sailed from Stockholm as the *Abraham Rydberg,* honoring the originator of the Abraham Rydberg Foundation, an organization dedicated to training cadets for the Swedish Merchant Marine. She operated mostly in the Australian grain trade, her cadet crews taking her back and forth between Scandinavian and British ports and the Australian grain loading centers. In 1939, while on a training cruise, she was unable to return to Stockholm because of the war and came to the United States. After being in New York for almost a year, she sailed to Newport News and loaded a full cargo of coal, sailing for South America on August 16, 1940, arriving in Santos late in November. The next year was spent training cadets while sailing between Santos and Boston.

On December 6, 1941, the day before Pearl Harbor, the *Abraham Rydberg* sailed again from Santos for Boston. The cargo consisted of 68,200 bags of fertilizer of cottonseed meal with 5 per cent castor pomace added; the total weight was 3,410 tons. After battling bad weather and unfavorable winds for three months and with the increased activity of the German submarines, the captain decided to bring the vessel to Baltimore instead of Boston. This was possible under the war risk clause of the bill of lading. Her captain, Oscar Malmberg, although only 30 years old, was an excellent sailor and the type to command a cadet ship.

She docked at the foot of Caroline Street at 1:30 p.m. on March 15, 1942 to discharge her cargo. The Clipper ship with her towering spars was an inspiration to see as she passed Fort McHenry moving into the inner harbor. The vessel had no winches, but had a donkey boiler which was used to raise her anchor and hoist the sails. The next day a swinging boom was rigged with rope falls, and with the help of the donkey boiler, the stevedores were able to start to discharge the cargo. This was a long and tedious job, as the bags that were beyond the hatch opening had to be brought by hand trucks to the square of the hatch. They were then loaded in slings of eight bags each and lifted by the swinging boom on to the dock. The cargo was finally discharged at noon on March 31, 1942. During the time the vessel was unloaded, the ship officers held daily classes for the 42 cadets on board. The mornings were spent repairing sails and renewing ropes, then the decks were swabbed until they actually glistened. After lunch, instructions were given on navigation, compass and use of the sextant. The cadets sailed the ship themselves with the help of the captain, the mates, the boatswain, the sailmaker and the carpenter. The cadets, between

Fells Point by A. Aubrey Bodine, 1930's

—*Peale Museum*

Fells Point by A. Aubrey Bodine, 1930's

16 and 20 years old, were ready for life at sea. Each had paid $200 for the privilege of sailing and also supplied his own bedding and personal effects. The cadets spent a year aboard the Clipper, during which time they would learn seamanship, navigation and more importantly, they would develop character, learn to depend on themselves and experience the value of unity.

On April 1, 1942, the *Abraham Rydberg* was moved from Fells Point to anchorage, where she stayed until January, 1943 when she was purchased by Julio Riberio Campos of Portugal for a reported $265,000 and renamed *Fox do Douro*. A careful survey had shown that her steel hull was sound. Outfitting her for sea, however, presented a problem to her owners and agents. Manila rope was hard to find and wire cable was equally scarce in a country at war. She was permitted to take aboard only what she actually needed for the voyage home and for every piece of new rope or cable going aboard, an old piece had to come ashore.

In April, 1943, she loaded in the port of Baltimore more than 204,000 packages of food destined to supplement the vitamin deficiencies in the diet of Allied war prisoners in Axis camps. As the ship got under way, the late A. Aubrey Bodine, a noted photographer for the *Sunday Sun,* finished a remarkable series of photographs. He had started taking pictures 60 days before as the Portuguese seamen were taking down the top gallant masts and yards. Since the ship was to pass through the Chesapeake and Delaware Canal to the Delaware Bay, they had to be lowered to permit passage under the canal bridges. After passing through the canal they were again raised at Ready Point on the Delaware River. Mr. Bodine was on board when she finally sailed for Portugal. He went a number of miles to sea to take photographs of the Portuguese seamen hoisting the sails on the old windjammer. Because it was wartime, Mr. Bodine had to have his photographs approved for publication by the Navy Department and the State Department. The unforgettable photographs of a passing era were finally published in the Sunday Metro-Gravure Section of the *Sunday Sun* on May 23, 1943. The *Abraham Rydberg* continued to sail between Portugal and South America until March 1945, when she was taken to Philadelphia to install two diesel engines. This ended her days as a sailing ship though for a while she sailed out of the port of Lisbon. In 1959 she was sold for scrap and eventually broken up in Italy.

In 1947 an attempt was made to reestablish a coastwise steamship line from Fells Point to Texas. The Norgulf Steamship Company operated from the foot of Caroline Street for two years but was forced to discontinue because of operating expenses. Between 1949 and 1955 the White Star fleet of the United Fruit Company used the same terminal to load their ships with supplies for the banana plantations in Central America.

In the 1950's the Mutual Chemical Company was acquired by the Allied Chemical Corporation which enlarged and modernized the manufacturing plant. Among the properties purchased for this expansion was the last shipyard in Fells Point. The Joseph Despeaux yard, established in 1794, at Philpot and Point Streets, had been operated by six different companies until purchased by the Chesapeake Marine Railway and Dry Dock Company in 1870. Chesapeake continued to operate it as a dry dock and repair yard for small bay sailing vessels and powerboats. It is ironic that the last shipyard to close in Fells Point was also the scene of the launching of the most controversial sailing ship in American history, the *Ann McKim.*

Abraham Rydberg
Built in 1892 in Glasgow, Scotland, the last full-rigged clipper ship
carrying cargo into the port

—Author's Collection

Another slowly vanishing breed in Fells Point was the Chesapeake Bay schooner captains. One of the last was also one of the most unforgettable. It was at the age of 15, after graduating from high school, that I first met John Tyler, captain of the two-masted schooner, *W. P. Ward*. He was six feet, weighing well over 200 pounds. His ruddy complexion was set off by his snow white hair, and he had a booming voice that made everyone jump when he started barking orders. He was born on March 11, 1859, at Dames Quarter, Somerset County, Maryland. At our first introduction, in July, 1931, Captain Tyler was 72, though the way he could move around the deck, jumping in and out of the yawl boat, one would guess his age as being in the early 50's.

During the 30's and early 40's, the *Ward* frequently loaded potash at Block Street Wharf which gave me the opportunity of spending many hours with Captain Tyler. I would skip lunch hour when the *Ward* was in port just to sit on the deck or in the cabin and listen to his tales of adventure and shipwrecks. He had a keen mind and a vivid memory, recalling the smallest detail of any incident. He was a stern captain and kept his schooner in tip-top shape. I still remember his summer attire, white shirt and tie and a hard straw hat. He had a great sense of humor which was proven by an incident which happened at the Block Street Wharf in 1935.

One morning while we were loading the *Ward*, I heard loud voices coming from the cabin. Suddenly the doors of the cabin flew open and two young deckhands ran to the rail and jumped to the wharf. They were followed by Captain Tyler, armed with a double-barrel shotgun. When the captain was sure the deckhands were well out of range, he let loose both barrels. Afterwards, with the widest grin on his face, he turned towards me and winked. The deckhands returned to the *Ward* hours later, visibly shaken. Even though I asked a number of times, Captain Tyler would never tell me what provoked this incident.

The captain once told me that as a young lad he knew he wanted to spend his life on the waters of the Chesapeake Bay. At 16 he was sailing his own small sloop. The next years were spent acquiring a knowledge of sailing, serving first as a deckhand and then as mate on bay schooners. In the early 1900's he was captain and part owner of the *Richard Cromwell*. During the spring and summer he would sail the schooner in the pineapple trade to and from the West Indies. He would load foodstuffs and general merchandise in Baltimore and sail to Eleuthera or Cat Islands in the Bahamas. His description of the beauty of those tropical islands and the natives was colorful and fascinating.

During the winter months he used the *Cromwell* as a buy boat during the oyster dredging season. The tongers would sell their oysters to a buy boat, anchored nearby, in order not to lose time in delivering to the packing houses themselves. When the *Cromwell* was loaded Captain Tyler would sell direct to the packing houses for a price slightly above what he paid the tongers. Little did I realize in 1940, when we unloaded the powerboat *Jeff* with canned goods from the Eastern Shore that its hull was originally the schooner *Richard Cromwell*.

Captain Tyler's pride and joy was the schooner *Emma Virginia* which he owned. This was built as a schooner with a centerboard and also had the characteristics of a pungy having a deep draft. The design resulted in a vessel which, according to Captain Tyler and the other dredgers who knew her, was one of the best boats on the Bay in heavy weather. The *Emma Virginia*, though, floundered off Deal Island

Chesapeake Marine Railway

Founded in 1868 by blacks. Isaac Myers and his brother George were
principals. The company failed in 1875

—Peale Museum

during a severe storm in 1915. Anchored while heavily loaded, she developed a leak and having a low freeboard, the high seas smashed her hatches. The pumps proved useless, but Captain Tyler and his mate, Charles Waller, who was also his son-in-law, stayed aboard manning the pumps until they had to be rescued from the rigging. The *Emma Virginia* was later blown up by the government because it was a hazard to navigation.

After losing the *Emma Virginia,* his next command was the schooner, *W. H. French,* owned by Harry Addison, who also owned several other schooners and rams. Mr. Addison, who transacted all his business at his home on Lanvale Street in Baltimore, was highly respected by Captain Tyler. During the next 15 years, the *French* was never without a charter and proved profitable for both Captain Tyler and Mr. Addison. Early in 1930, Mr. Addison died and his interests were sold including the *W. H. French.*

Captain Tyler found himself without a schooner, although he had several charters for full cargoes. He was unable to obtain the schooner, *Clemmie Travers,* so he took command of the *L. E. Williams* which had been anchored in the Canton flats for several years. Captain Tyler knew the *Williams* needed some repair work but he was forced to meet one of his charters immediately. He berthed the schooner at the Standard Oil dock in Canton to load drums of gasoline consigned to Deal Island. The loading was completed late in the afternoon of October 4, 1930, and the captain set sail for the Eastern Shore. During the early hours of the next morning the *Williams* sprung a leak as they neared Sharps Island. With the help of the mate and his nephew, Julius Tyler, the captain tried to keep the schooner afloat by using all the available pumps. Seeing that they were fighting a losing battle, he next tried to beach the schooner on Travers Point. When this didn't work, Captain Tyler, noting the perilous condition of the schooner, ordered everyone to abandon the ship. As the three men cleared the schooner in the yawl boat, the *Williams* capsized and sank.

Several months later Captain Tyler took command of the schooner, *W. P. Ward,* owned by Farmers and Planters Company of Salisbury, Maryland. Her previous captain had suddenly become ill and died aboard the *Ward* while docked at Salisbury. He was Charles Waller, Captain Tyler's son-in-law, who had served as his mate on the *Emma Virginia.* For the next 12 years, Captain Tyler, with his son Lacy as mate, continued to sail the *Ward* from Baltimore and Norfolk carrying raw materials to the Farmers & Planters fertilizer plant in Salisbury. The *Ward,* built in 1882 in Cambridge, Maryland, was beginning to shown signs of age. During World War II, there was a great demand for sailing craft to carry cargoes between Florida and the West Indies. Farmers & Planters sold the *Ward* in 1943 to A. D. Bessemer of Miami and later that year the old schooner sailed out of the Chesapeake Bay forever.

Captain Tyler retired from life at sea to his home at Chance, Maryland to join Ella, his wife of 59 years. The next seven years he enjoyed the simple things of life, taking care of his vegetable garden and the flower beds which surrounded the house. He died in 1950, at the age of 91 and is buried in the Rock Creek Cemetery in Chance. Mrs. Tyler died in 1955 in her 97th year.

I will always remember Captain John Tyler, a typical Eastern Shore sailing master. They were a breed of their own, driving their vessels through fair weather and foul.

Nine of the original houses in Fells Point were torn down in the early 1950's

Schooner W. H. French with Captain Tyler

and replaced by a one-story warehouse. These houses were located on the south side of the 1600 block Thames Street (1621 to 1637). Some historians claim that 1621 was the original home of William Fell, built in 1730. They feel the entrance of the Fell mansion fronted on Lancaster Street and that Thames Street was cut through some years later. These facts are based on an ordinance passed April 1, 1973 which provided for the raising of the bed of Thames Street 21 inches. The ordinance stated the break in the grade of Thames Street was to take place in the east wall of the old Fell mansion, making the exact point the northeast corner of the building.

In 1960, the plan for the East-West expressway route was shifted from the northside of the business district of Baltimore to the southside and along the waterfront through Fells Point. As soon as this plan was announced the commercial activities in Fells Point began to decline at an alarming rate. By 1964, a number of canning factories had closed or moved to nearby counties. Marine activity was practically non-existent, with only an occasional vessel berthed at the foot of Bond Street discharging sugar or newsprint. In 230 years, Fells Point had made a complete cycle, from a booming shipbuilding center and port to a deteriorated section of Baltimore.

The Renaissance Years

1965 . . .

Sunday, November 7, 1965 was the beginning of a new era. On that day, Mrs. A. Murray Fisher of Ruxton decided to ride through Fells Point, a section which fascinated her. As she rode down Thames Street, a "for sale" sign in the window of a house at 1732 caught her eye. Curious, Mrs. Fisher stopped and inspected the house. She was so excited about the possibility of restoring it that in ten days she bought the house.

During 1966, the fight to alter the route of the highway through Fells Point was led by Baltimore Heritage, Inc., a non-profit architectural preservation organization headed by Mrs. Fisher and Thomas H. Ward. Mr. Ward was the city councilman from the second district which included Bolton Hill, an old section of the city which was successfully being restored.

Mr. Ward introduced an ordinance on June 13 to move the route of the highway a block north to save the historic buildings on Thames, Lancaster and Shakespeare Streets. The plan met with mixed reactions as this proposed route would destroy St. Stanislaus Church. A month later Mayor Theodore McKeldin announced that the city was examining a plan to move 30 or 40 200-year-old houses out of the highway path to a landfill next to the Recreation Pier.

In December, 1966, informal meetings were held by a few concerned Fells Pointers to discuss the routes. In February, 1967, this group organized The Society for the Preservation of Federal Hill, Montgomery Street and Fells Point. Federal Hill was included because it faced destruction by the proposed Southwest Boulevard. Mrs. Fisher was elected president.

The society was organized to find the means of preserving and developing the two districts as a living heritage of the city's history and to bring to the attention of the public the historic value of these old neighborhoods. But the first order of business was to try and save the community from the highway system.

A public hearing was held at City Hall on February 14, 1967 to discuss the merits of the East-West Highway. The opponents of the plan were again led by Councilman Ward, now a member of the Fells Point Preservation Society. The debate between the expressway planners and the preservationists became so heated that Chairman William Donald D. Schaefer closed the hearing.

The fight by the preservationists had attracted nationwide attention. On April 10, the *New York Times* declared:

"A planned eight-lane elevated highway threatens to destroy Fells Point, a harborside neighborhood settled in 1730 and recently rediscovered by persons lured by its quaint sidestreets and old buildings. Under pressure from state and Federal officials, condemnation procedures have already begun in nearby neighborhoods through which the super-road will stretch. But a handful of property owners hope to save Fells Point and to lure young people to establish residences that can be painted and refurnished for their historic and architectural interest."

In defiance of the threat of condemnation, at least 15 buildings were purchased during 1966 and 1967 by persons who were convinced the highway would be diverted north of the Point. The new owners began to restore their homes and talked of Fells Point becoming "another Georgetown, only better."

On Monday, May 29, the city council passed the condemnation ordinance by a vote of 20 to 1, only Councilman Ward dissenting. The ordinance was approved only after the council beat down an unexpected bid by the First District (Fells Point) councilman to tack on an amendment which would have required the city and state to pay more than fair market value to owners of all homes in the path of any expressway in the city. The amendment finally died on a 13 to 8 roll call.

At the June meeting of the preservation society it was decided to try to have Fells Point designated as a Historic District by applying to the U. S. Department of the Interior for National Register under the Historical Preservation Act of 1966. A survey committee, headed by Jack Gleason and Robert Eney, prepared the necessary papers including maps, aerial photographs and close-ups of certain houses along with the descriptive sheets. On September 12 the report was presented to the Division of History, U. S. Department of Interior. The committee was informed that Stewart L. Udall, Secretary of Interior, would make a decision in November.

To help raise money to continue its fight, the society held the first Fells Point Fun Festival on Sunday, October 8, at the foot of Broadway. It was a tremendous success and is now an annual affair with an average attendance of over 50,000.

The society was pleased when an article appeared in a magazine published by Urban America describing the Fells Point-Federal Hill section of Baltimore as "the only impelling aspect of an otherwise unimposing city."

On January 3, 1968 during a heated meeting between the society and the road builders, Jerome B. Wolff, chairman of the State Roads Commission, announced that the expressway route would not be changed. He softened this somewhat by promising that the state would not begin buying the 18th century houses in Fells Point until a report on the area was received from the urban design concept team.

Mr. Wolff conceded that the path through Fells Point and Federal Hill "may not be the best solution." 'I admit the best solution would be to take it away," he said. "It isn't only esthetics that solve these problems," he reminded the preservationists. "It is also the hard political realities of life."

Regardless of the seriousness of the situation a bit of humor seemed to arise. In a letter to Mr. Wolff, Senator Julian L. Lapides (second district, Baltimore) noted that "Who's Afraid of Jerome Wolff?" buttons were selling in some areas at "black market prices" and that these buttons were outselling, three to one, buttons that read "Save Federal Hill and Fells Point." Senator Lapides added, "I am not sure what this shows, but I guess that we can each draw our own conclusions." He concluded, "I am thinking of setting up a booth outside of 300 West Preston Street," the State Roads Commission office, and "bootlegging" the buttons, normally sold by the society for 15 cents, for $1. Shortly thereafter, he received a request for a dollar's worth of buttons. It came from Mrs. Jerome Wolff.

Other groups throughout the city began to realize the importance of the fight the society was waging against the highway system. On August 3, more than 30 civil rights, neighborhood, preservation and professional groups met to organize neighborhood support and bring pressure to bear on city, state and federal officials involved in the planning.

During the fall a number of meetings were held between the U. S. Department of Transportation, the State Roads Commission and city officials to determine the most advantageous route for the expressway. On December 23, Mayor Thomas D'Alesandro announced that he favored the route across Baltimore known as 3-A.

The decision represented a victory for the preservationists who sought to avoid an inner harbor crossing which would have taken the road along Federal Hill and for various civic groups which had sought to avoid damage to Rosemont, a stable black neighborhood in West Baltimore. But Fells Point remained in the road's path. Despite the holidays, gloom settled over the neighborhood and there was a noticeable lack of celebrating the New Year.

Fells Point, which had withstood the enemy in the early 1800's was in danger in the 1960's. The Mayor and city councilmen were not against its destruction and the Design Concept Team, which proposed alternative routes in Rosemont and Federal Hill, had no other proposals for Fells Point. The only hope left was in the hands of the preservation society and the people themselves.

It suffered another blow in February when the U. S. Department of Interior refused to declare it a historic area. The setback did not discourage the society. A new survey and historic study was prepared and presented to the Maryland Historic Trust for designation as a National Registered Historic District. This was approved on March 28, 1969, the first such designation in Maryland.

> The Natural Register of Historic Places, 1969, declares, "Fells Point, a national registered historic district, is bounded on the north by Aliceanna Street, on the east by Wolfe Street, on the south by the harbor and on the west by Dallas Street. Fells Point is a harborside, residential community that encompasses approximately 75 acres in the eastern section of Baltimore. The character of its townscape is set by groupings of small 2½ story houses which were the homes of seamen, ship's carpenters, sailmakers and other artisans involved in the port activities. These smaller houses are interspersed with occasional larger, more elaborate 3½ story houses which were the homes of the shipyard owners, prosperous merchants, and sea captains."

To familiarize Baltimoreans with the importance of Fells Point, the preservation society held a 20-block walking tour on March 31, 1969 advertised as "one of the largest colonial workingman's communities still in existence." The turnout exceeded expectations.

On April 7 a suit was filed in federal court against federal and state highway officials, calling the selection of the expressway route "arbitrary and capricious." The plaintiffs in the action, filed by Norman P. Ramsey, were 23 residents of Fells Point.

Steele House before renovation

Built in 1790's, the house is noted for interior woodwork

—Fells Point Historical Society

Steele House after renovation

—Fells Point Historical Society

The suit claimed that "many of the existing buildings and structures in the Fells Point area had been declared historic sites of local, state and national significance by local, state and federal authorities."

The Baltimore chapter of the American Institute of Architects opposed construction of the expressway. In a resolution it described Fells Point as "the oldest and architecturally most historic district of Baltimore, and the last remaining residential waterfront community in the city." It added that the neighborhood is "on the threshold of economic and architectural rehabilitation entirely promoted and financed by private enterprise, which will increase the flow of business, trade and revenue dollars to the city's economy."

In October the Urban Design Concept Team announced it had completed four alternative expressway proposals for Fells Point, none involving construction of a surface road. The report said that the proposal for an underground East-West expressway through Fells Point would probably gain the most public favor, but it would also be the most expensive.

By the spring of 1970, the city had acquired 80 properties in Fells Point despite the fact that there had been no final approval of funding from the federal government; city money was used. Some of the former property owners stayed on as renters. Through the combined efforts of the society and the city relocation office, nine houses were rented by new residents interested in the preservation of the area.

After a speech at Johns Hopkins on April 22, John Volpe, Secretary of Transportation, promised the preservationists that he would come to Baltimore to review the situation and meet the groups opposing the expressway. On June 25, he met with concerned groups at the community center in the 2200 block of Edmondson Avenue. Mrs. Fisher and Mr. Eney told Mr. Volpe that the highway would ruin an irreplaceable historical district. Mr. Volpe said he had issued an administrative order to the effect that "no family will have their house torn down until they are relocated to a decent place to live." Mr. Volpe took back to Washington a large volume, prepared by Mr. Eney and Mr. Gleason, on the historic character of Fells Point and its potential.

To help defray mounting legal expenses the society held the first Harbor Ball on June 6 in the ballroom of the Recreation Pier.

The Maryland State Society Daughters of the American Colonists presented Fells point with a historic marker, dedicated and erected on September 20 on the edge of the harbor at the foot of Broadway. It reads:

> Fells Point . . . A colonial maritime community established 1726 by William Fell, shipbuilder of Lancashire, England. In this area were built more than six hundred ships from the colonial era through the Civil War. Birthplace of the U. S. Frigate Constellation and home port of the Famous Baltimore Clippers.

Ironically, two mistakes were made in the inscription. It was Edward Fell, not William, who arrived in Baltimore in 1726, and William Fell founded Fells Point in 1730.

For the next nine months the "battle of the expressway" was at a standstill. On May 14, 1971, the Interstate Division of the State Roads Department submitted their "4F" report to the U. S. Department of Transportation in Washington which attempted to justify the route through Fells Point. ("4F refers to Sec. 4 Subsec. F.

of the National Highway Act of 1968 which says that highways funded by the federal government cannot take park or historical sites unless there is no prudent or feasible alternative.) Several weeks later the report was returned with the notation "incomplete."

Under advice by legal counsel for "The Citizen Group of Fells Point" suit against the federal government, the society prepared its own report which: 1) showed alternative routes were never seriously considered for the proposed Fells Point road, 2) illustrated the area's historic worth, and 3) clarified the position of eastern industries. In the meantime, Congress passed the Environmental Policy Act, which made it necessary for the State Roads Commission to show how the proposed road would effect the areas through which it would pass, in 14 different aspects.

As the year ended the society's fight against the road was beginning to show encouraging results.

On January 1, 1972, William D. Schaefer was sworn in as Mayor of Baltimore. He had been involved in the highway hearings for the last five years. He was determined to complete the expressway system through Baltimore. During January he held what was billed as a "full briefing" on the background of the cross-city expressway for the benefit of the new city council. This turned out to be an administration "pitch" as to why the council and the public should accept the inevitability of expressways through the city.

The first Historic Harbor House Tour of Federal Hill and Fells Point was held March 26. The tour gave the 355 people who attended the opportunity to observe in detail the preservation work accomplished on the 12 houses on display. On April 1 the Baltimore City Bicentennial Committee announced that it was considering Fells Point as the center of the city's activity during the 200th birthday celebration of the U. S. A.

The society announced the establishment of the Historic Fells Point and Federal Hill Fund, Inc., a non-profit, tax-exempt organization incorporated to operate exclusively for educational and charitable purposes in preserving both registered national historic districts.

In May Mayor Schaefer announced his plan to proceed with the construction of the 3-A expressway system including I-83 through Fells Point. The society responded with a release reiterating its opposition.

It was not until the spring of 1973 that the society scored its first victory. In an April 3 decision, Judges Roszel Thomsen and James R. Miller refused the government's request that the suit, Lukowski vs Volpe, opposing construction of the expressway, be thrown out. The judges chided the government attorneys for wanting to "knock down houses and dig holes" before a specific route had been approved by the federal government. The suit would now be tried in court.

Councilwoman Barbara Mikulski, (first district Baltimore), introduced three anti-highway bills. A public hearing was held on June 20 and in keeping with the hard line of Mayor Schaefer the bills were defeated. The city engaged the firm of Per Hall Associates of Montreal to study the feasibility of having the road submerged into a tunnel under the shoreline of Fells Point. Simultaneously, Zollman Associates, Inc., had undertaken consideration of nine alternatives for the routing of the road through Fells Point.

A committee from various Fells Point organizations met with Robert Embry,

Brown's Wharf

A waterfront warehouse that has been in operation for over 150 years.
Rukert Terminals acquired the facilities in 1947. The museum is housed
in the building on the left

—Photograph by Harry Connolly

Baltimore City Commissioner of Housing and Community Development, to hire a firm of architectural planners to work with the community to formulate a comprehensive, coordinated plan for the future development of the area.

The society acquired its first property in the summer of 1973 when it purchased the Robert Long house at 812 South Ann Street (circa 1765). Built by a Cecil County businessman in 1792, it was recorded as an old house. The society did not have sufficient funds for its purchase so the members of the Board of Directors advanced the money, to be repaid in five years. In November, the Maryland Chapter of the Daughters of the American Revolution announced it would furnish the first floor as its statewide Bicentennial project.

During the summer of 1974 Mayor Schaefer announced the retention of Louis Sauer Associates, a consulting firm experienced in urban landscape and design work, for the proposed revitalization of the Fells Point area and representatives of community groups and organizations formed the Fells Point Planning Council.

Lengthy hearings were held in January 1975 on the nine route proposals for I-83. Witnesses for the preservation society and the historic fund voiced their choice for "no road" at all, despite the city's preference for alignment no. 9, which would have the highway pass under the harbor off Fells Point. Continuing delay, lack of communication from the city and state, and city neglect in the section marked for condemnation had taken a serious toll.

The society felt that as soon as road condemnation lines were lifted, private developers would move in and begin tearing down and building before the master plan was approved by the city council. It was decided to have Fells Point declared an Urban Renewal Area and appropriate legislation was introduced on August 4 at a special meeting of the city council. This would give the city Department of Housing and Community Development (HCD) and the Fells Point Planning Council veto power over major changes in property, changes not in line with the neighborhood plan prepared by the Fells Point Planning Council.

In spite of the threat of the expressway a number of restorations have been completed:

The Captain Steele House—931 Fell Street, Dr. and Mrs. Walter R. Hepner, Jr. Built in the 1790s, it is noted for its superb interior woodwork. It is an excellent example of a large 18th century town house built for a prosperous citizen. It has been included in the Historic American Buildings Survey and in one of the Winterhur portfolios.

The Captain Pitt House—910 Fell Street, Dr. and Mrs. A. Murray Fisher. Built in the late 18th century as a two-and-a-half story building for a wealthy ship captain. The present full third floor was added much later. The house contains much of the original woodwork, such as the hallway arch and most of the stairway. The second floor drawing room front has the original mantelpiece.

The John Smyth House—1600 Shakespeare Street, Mrs. Winnie Krieger. Built about 1777 on property purchased from Ann Fell by John Smyth who lived here with his family and two slaves. It has many remarkable features such as a cooking fireplace and bread ovens. It still carries a ground rent payable in shillings.

The House with the Red Door—1815 Thames Street, Mr. Robert Eney and Mr. John Gleason.

Originally two separate buildings, typical workingmen's houses of the early 19th century. Antique and reproduction paneling and trim have been combined to recreate an interior architectural style of the 18th century. The staircase of long grain pine was brought from a colonial house in Delaware.

Studio of Miss Stephanie Scuris—937 Fell Street.

Formerly a warehouse, this has been adapted to the needs of an active sculptress and artist. Miss Scuris works in metal, wood, stone and other media on creations that have won her international recognition.

707 S. Regester Street—Rev. Robert L. Young.

This little 2½ story wooden house is sheathed with wide cypress boards up to 16 inches in width—with a beaded edge. The house shows its 18th century origins in the construction methods as well as in the existing fireplaces, doors, trim and wide floor boards. The kitchen has been reconstructed. A wide variety of early fine china and bottles have been dug up in the yard. At least ten other wooden houses of this type still stand in the area.

727 S. Ann Street—Mr. and Mrs. Herbert Zientek.

Dating from the late 18th century it closely resembles the Captain Steele house. The roof with its dormer windows and huge chimney was removed about 50 years ago, giving the house a more modern appearance. The present owners have restored the beautiful Flemish bond brick work. The house was occupied in 1814 by Sheppard Church Leakin and his wife Elizabeth. He was a captain in the 38th U. S. Infantry and served throughout the War of 1812. He was injured while helping to erect the fortifications on Loundenslagers Hill (Patterson Park). Though not in command of his troops, he was able to be present during the bombardment of Fort McHenry. He was a member of the committee that received General Lafayette during his visit to Fells Point in 1824. A printer and publisher by trade, Leakin was the proprietor of the Baltimore *Chronicle* which had offices on Market Square at the foot of Broadway. He also served as Mayor of Baltimore from 1838 to 1840.

1624 Lancaster Street—Mr. M. L. Eney and Mr. George Weissmann.

The roof has been raised, making a full third floor, on this house that was built about 1785 as a 2½ story dwelling. The early records are not clear as to the owner or builder but many different people and businesses have occupied it during the last 190 years. It was operated as a barber shop during the 1930's. The house has two corner fireplaces on the first floor and original mantlepieces, doors and trim. The kitchen, which was originally detached from the house, is brickfloored with a small fireplace.

Many other houses are still in the early stages of restoration.

In the middle of Fells Point, at 1617 Thames Street, stands Brown's Wharf, a waterfront warehouse which has been in continuous operation for over 150 years.

In 1839 George Brown, son of Alexander Brown, decided that Baltimore needed a new pier with supporting warehouses due to the tremendous growth of the coffee and flour trade. On May 25, 1840 he purchased a parcel of land in Fells Point which included the waterfront property from the foot of Broadway west to the foot of Bond Street. This was made up of a number of small wharves which were owned or previously owned by some of the most prominent merchants. These included Hugh Thompson, Robert Oliver, Thomas Sheppard and James and Joseph Biays. The first mention of the property was a deed dated December 28, 1780 between William Fell, the grantor, and John German and Thomas Dorsey, the grantees, for the term of 99 years with the benefit of renewal forever and under the clear yearly rent of ten pounds sterling.

When George Brown bought the property there were two warehouses on the premises which were built by James and Joseph Biays in 1822. The two are virtually untouched and are still being used after 150 years. The buildings consist of three floors and a loft with an extreme roof pitch to eliminate snow accumulation. The west building measures 80 feet by 35 feet and the east building 50 feet by 48 feet. Connected to the east building is a one-story annex, 23 feet by 48 feet, which was used to house slaves. Only the finest materials were used in the construction of the warehouses. The bricks were imported from England and the slate for the roofs came from Wales. The 18 inch by 12 inch beams throughout the warehouses are Georgia pine and are held in place by wooden plugs. Some of the beams are charred, evidence of a small fire which occurred in 1848. The brick walls are 20 inches thick and the lintels over the doorways are of granite, 8 inches thick and 7 feet long. The Georgia pine roof joints are handhewed. On the top floors iron rods run from an iron plate on the outside walls along the beams and are connected by a turn buckle; this kept the walls from swaying in high winds. The small fixtures which held the lanterns are still in place on all floors. Each floor is connected by a closed wooden stairway and in the center of each room is a 4 foot by 3 foot trap door. The loft of the west building is unusual, with a ceiling height from 19 feet on the west side tapering to zero on the east side. It is possible this was once used as a sail loft.

Graffiti was just as popular in the 1800's as it is today. Writings on the beams and walls include "J. Emerson 1860," "Bark May Queen docked Brown's Wharf December 7, 1870," "For Gov. John Lee Carroll, for Mayor Col. F. C. Latrobe, for Sheriff Mills." Some of the writing is faded.

Immediately after acquiring the property, George Brown constructed a new cone shaped pier, 275 feet long on the north side and 304 feet on the south side. The width on the shore end was 95 feet tapering to 20 on the outer end. Here Clipper ships unloaded coffee from Brazil or loaded flour for the return trip south. And Brown's Wharf was the terminal for the Havana-New Orleans Steamship Line.

George Brown died in 1859 and ownership of the wharf was transferred to his wife Isabella. As business continued to boom during the next 25 years the Brown interests decided to build two additional warehouses. These were three stories high fronting on Thames Street. The warehouses, finished in 1868, were separated by a 17 foot covered roadway which ran from Thames Street, between the four buildings, to the cone-shaped pier. This was an innovation, the first in the port of Baltimore, and enabled the warehouses to operate regardless of weather conditions.

As the 20th century approached, the future of Brown's Wharf became cloudy with the loss of the coffee trade to New York and the arrival of new large

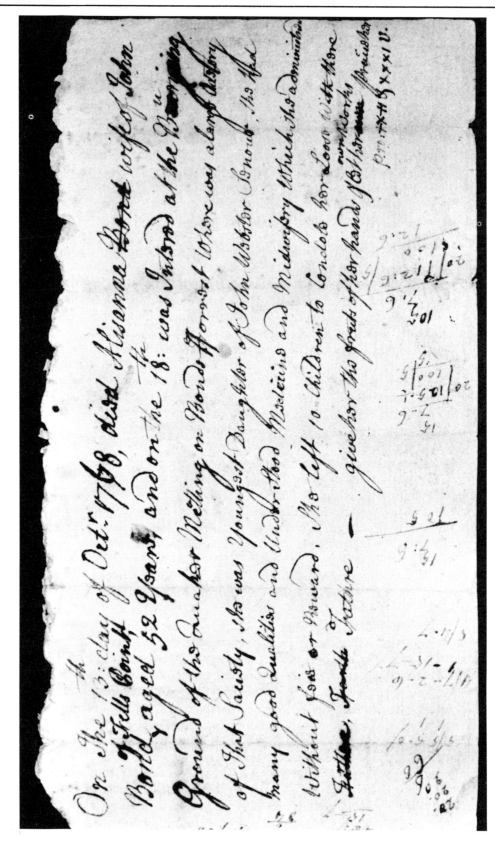

Bond and Fell Papers
Alisanna Bond's Obituary—October 13, 1768

Ulverstone February 14th 1766

Then Sold by William Myrin of Whitehaven (by Virtue of a Letter of Attorney from Edward Fell of Maryland in North America) to Roger Fisher of Ulverstone, All that Customary Estate held under Sir John Pennington Bar. as Lord thereof, being of the Yearly Customary Rent of Twenty Eight Shillings & Eight Pence, Situate at Trinkell in the Manor of Pennington & County Palatine of Lancaster for the Sum of Two Hundred and Ninety Pounds. ———

The Premises are to be Subject to a Rectory Rent of Eleven pence and the above mentioned Customary rent of £1.8.8 & the Customary Fines Dues Duties & Services ———

The Purchaser to have a good Title according to the Custom, to be prepared at his own Expense and to enter into immediate possession from this day. ———

The Purchaser agrees to pay & discharge immediately the Sum of Sixty Nine pounds & Two Shillings a Mortgage on the Premises to Edward Taylor & Miles Dodgson as by Account this day settled with them by William Myrin, And to pay to the P. William Myrin On or before the 14th day of May next the further Sum of Two Hundred & Twenty Pounds & Eighteen Shillings the residue of the Purchase Money, having then a good Title made to him of the Premises. In Witness to this agreement the Parties have set their hands this 14th day of February 1766. ———

Witnesses present at the making this agreement & the Parties subscribing their Names. ——
Thos. Ireland
Jas. Spedding

110 - 9 - 0

Wm Myrin

Rogd Fisher

Bond and Fell Papers

Letter from England regarding Fell's Property—February 14, 1766

London ye: 24th April 1766

Mr: John Bond

Sir

I am fav: with your Letter dat: ye 20th Sepr Last, with 2 Hhd: Tobacco by ye Peggy George Woodle Master, Inclosed is the account of Sales Nett Proceeds Nine Pounds two Shillings, Fourpence, which being Deducted from £12.12.0 Edward Fells Bill you order me to charge to you, Leaves you in my Debt, Three = Pounds, Nine Shillings, Two Pence, The above Ship is to Load for me this year In Bush: or Bta[...]. Bryan Philpot may order, it not Agt:[...] you an opportunity of Letting with the Master about the Freight also I agree it will be to your Liking to continue your Business with me. you may be Assured I will take great care to serve you well as I shall with Friend you may be so Kind as to recommend. being with great Esteem

Sir your most H'ble Servant
John Philpot

Bond and Fell Papers

Agreement to build a house on Aliceanna Street—July 13, 1782

—Browns Wharf Museum

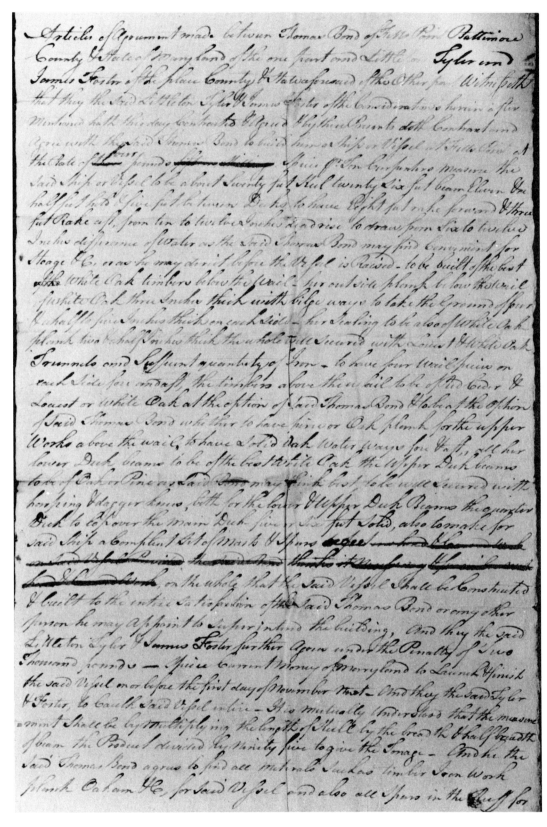

Bond and Fell Papers

Agreement to build a boat in Fells Point—April 28, 1783

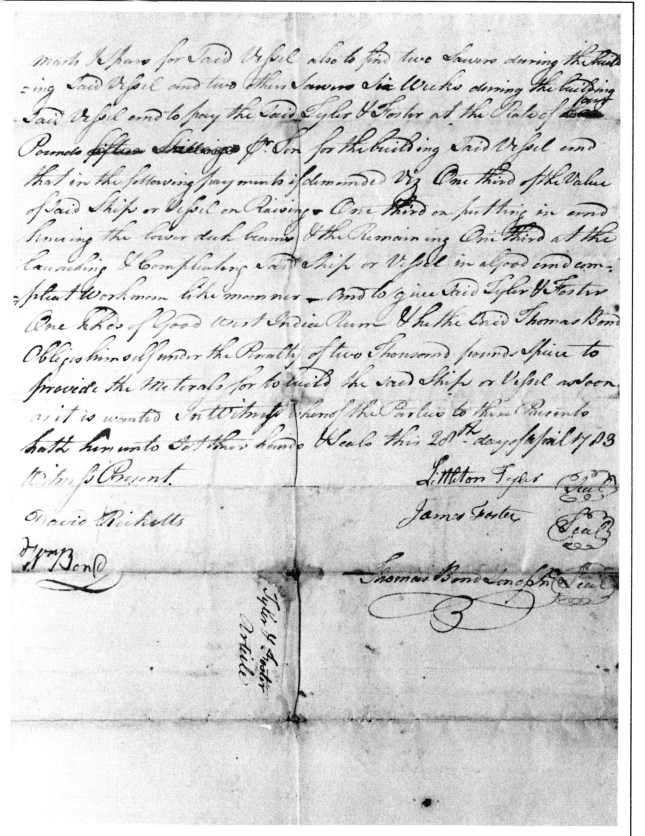

Masts & Spars for Said Vessel also to find two Sawers during the build
=ing Said Vessel and two other Sawers Six Weeks during the building
Said Vessel and to pay the Said Tyler & Foster at the Rate of four
Pounds fifteen Shillings pr Ton for the building Said Vessel and
that in the following payments if demanded viz One third of the Value
of Said Ship or Vessel on Raising, One third on putting in and
Securing the lower deck beams & the Remaining One third at the
Launching & Compleating said Ship or Vessel in a good and com-
=pleat Workman like manner — And to give Said Tyler & Foster
One Rhod of Good West India Rum & he the said Thomas Bond
Obliges himself under the Penalty of two Thousand pounds Spece to
provide the Materals for to build the said Ship or Vessel as soon
as it is wanted In Witness whereof the Parties to these Presents
hath hereunto Set their hands & Seals this 28th day of April 1783

Witness Present.   Litteton Tyler   (Seal)

David Ricketts   James Foster   (Seal)

Wm Bond
                                       Thomas Bond Joseph   (Seal)

Tyler & Foster
Article

Bond and Fell Papers
Agreement to build a boat in Fells Point—April 28, 1783

steamers requiring longer piers and deeper water. In 1890, the *Grey Eagle,* a coffee Clipper of the Whitridge fleet, was the last vessel to unload at the terminal.

In the meantime, on the death of Isabella Brown, the property passed to her son, George S. Brown, and then to his son, Alexander Brown of Mondawmin. On September 4, 1897, he merged all activities at this location under the name of the Brown Warehouse Company. For the next seven years the Brown Warehouse Company continued to operate the complex for the storage of canned goods packed in Fells Point. On November 30, 1904, the property was sold to the Western Maryland Railway. In 1920, the pier, which had become antiquated, was partially removed, leaving only a small section for loading and unloading of lighters. During the Depression business continued to lag; in 1939 only 74 tons of merchandise were handled. To stimulate business parts of the property were rented to Fells Point merchants. On May 25, 1947, the Western Maryland Railway sold the complex to Rukert Terminals Corporation. Rukert modernized the facilities without disturbing the original building, and has continued using this property for the storage of waterborne commodities.

When the Department of the Interior registered Fells Point as a National Historic District, plans were made to turn one the original buildings into a waterfront warehouse museum and it was officially opened by Mayor Schaefer on March 20, 1976.

The museum features a 10 x 12 foot map model of Fells Point as it appeared in the 18th century. Displays also include ship models, old records, coffee mugs and photographs of vessels which were built here. Life-size displays of work material and work methods of the 19th century are exhibited.

In midsummer Louis Sauer Associates published its report on the first phase of the Fells Point Planning Study.

The report suggests three alternate plans chosen to gain insight into the action various interest groups, both living in and outside of Fells Point, want.

"NO CHANGE"—People are tired of change and its long process and talk and general rabble rousing. They've lived happily in their community for years, are quite self sufficient, and want no more interruptions. Fells Point has been a comfortable community and if it is left alone some people would be satisfied with their present living and working environment. The need for a highway is not strong enough to cause further trouble.

"ONWARD"—The waterfront should become a central theme of the area, with its potential economic attractions. Existing business should be replaced with tourist-related enterprises to enhance Fells Point's visitor market and would extend the character of the Inner Harbor into the area. The Historic District would be protected from commercial intrusion.

"LIVE"—The community and the city respect the diversity of interest that is unique to Fells Point. These interests are formed by long term residents of the community, new people moving into Fells Point, and the tourists who steadily visit and shop the area. To protect these values, the community and city must decide together to institute the entire range of planning controls and incentives, and act to create a new environment.

Regardless of the outcome, one must admire the unyielding fight the small group of Fells Pointers has waged against the expressway. They have met every challenge from the federal, state and city governments with the same determination and fortitude the early settlers exhibited during the Revolutionary War and the War of 1812. The society's membership has increased to over 500 and its fund-raising functions—The Historic Harbor House Tour, Harbor Ball and Fun Festival receive widespread support.

Fort McHenry

Epilogue

The shipbuilders of Fells Point performed an immeasurable service for their country by helping develop both the Baltimore Clipper and the American Clipper. The vessels built here were among the finest in the world and gave Baltimore the start it needed to become the great port which it is today.

Baltimoreans should be proud of their heritage. That heritage is beautifully elucidated in this article written by a prominent patriot at the end of the War of 1812:

> During the whole struggle against an inveterate foe, they did all they could to aid and strengthen the hands of the general government, and generally took the lead in fitting out efficient privateers and letters of marque to annoy and distress the enemy, and even to "'beard the old lion in his den," for it is well known that their privateers captured many English vessels at the very mouths of their own ports in the British channel.
>
> When their own beautiful city was attacked by a powerful fleet and army, how nobly did they defend themselves against the hand of the spoiler! The whole venom of the modern Goths seemed concentrated against the Baltimoreans, for no other reason but that they had too much spirit to submit to insult and tyrannical oppression. Many of the eastern people made a grand mistake in counting on the magnanimity of the British nation to do them justice by mild and persuasive arguments. In making these remarks in praise of Baltimore, I do not mean to disparage the noble patriotism of many other cities of our glorious Union, but I do mean to say, that if the same spirit that fired the hearts and souls of the Baltimoreans, had evinced itself throughout our entire country, it would have saved every American heart much pain and mortification, and would, in my opinion, have shortened the war. For while the English believed we were a divided people, they were slow to relinquish their unreasonable demands. With these obvious reasons, can anyone possessed of the least knowledge of human nature, believe there can ever be any real friendship between an English Aristocrat, a High-Church Tory, and an American Republican; the very idea of such friendship is preposterous to the last degree. It therefore follows, that we have only to rely upon our own strength and union, to repel aggression from whatever quarter it may come. Would the English, if they had succeeded in taking Baltimore, have shown more mercy in sparing it than they did Washington? I have no patience with such fallacious reasoning.

The author of the above article was in Baltimore shortly after the English had retreated. At Fort McHenry he saw the American flag, with its beautiful stars and stripes, waving gracefully in the breeze. The impression made upon him was undeniable. He did not attempt to describe the feeling because it had been better expressed in Francis Scott Key's immortal words of the "Star Spangled Banner."

Shipbuilders in Fells Point

Years	Name	Location
1731–1746	William Fell	*Thames Street*
1750–1762	Mark Alexander	*Thames St. East of Caroline St.*
1765	Benjamin Nelson	*Philpot Street*
1773–1795	George Wells	*Thames & Bond Sts.*
1779–1804	James Morgan	*Fells Street*
1794–1820	Joseph Despeaux	*Philpot & Point Sts.*
1795–1801	John Steele & Thomas Lambdin	*Fells Street*
1796–1803	Louis DeRochbrune	*Thames St. East of Caroline St.*
1796–1833	William Price	*East end of Thames St.*
1799–1801	Joseph Caverly	*Philpot St. West of Point St.*
1800–1804	James Cordery	*Philpot St. West of Thames St.*
1803–1815	Thomas Kemp	*Washington & Aliceanna Sts.*
1803–1816	Joshua Willil	*Thames St.*
1803–1818	William Parsons	*East end of Lancaster St.*
1804	James Biays	*Thames St.*
1804–1810	Stephen Berillant	*Foot of Bond St.*
1814–1817	William F. Inloes	*East end of Thames St.*
1814–1819	Jos. Robson & Jos. Denny	*East end of Lancaster St.*
1814–1833	Samuel C. Kinnard	*Philpot & Point Sts.*
1816	Thomas Kemp & Geo. Gardner	*Washington & Aliceanna Sts.*
1816–1822	G. Gardner & Jos. Robson	*Washington & Aliceanna Sts.*
1816–1817	Mathew Cook & Gasper Lioni	*Thames St. Near Broadway*
1816–1817	Robert Robinson	*East end of Lancaster St.*
1816–1821	James Riggin	*East end of Lancaster St.*
1817–1822	Robert Cooper	*Foot of Wolfe St.*
1818–1827	Flannigan & Beacham	*East end of Lancaster St.*
1822–1860	George & William Gardner	*Washington & Aliceanna Sts.*
1820–1828	Anthony Despeaux	*Philpot & Point Sts.*
1825	Etienne Berillant	*Foot of Bond St.*
1827–1830	Robb & Donaldson	*Thames St.*
1827–1841	Andrew & Benjamin Flannigan	*East end of Lancaster St.*
1828–1831	Thomas Bailey	*Philpot St. West of Thames St.*
1829–1831	Basil L. Smith	*East end of Aliceanna St.*
1829–1838	Auld & Harrison	*Block St. near Point St.*
1830–1866	John Robb Co.	*Thames St.*
1831–1834	Kinnard & Williamson	*Philpot & Point Sts.*
1831–1834	Richard Lawrence	*East end of Lancaster St.*
1831–1837	John Richardson	*Foot of Ann St.*

Shipbuilders in Fells Point

Years	Name	Location
1831–1842	Bailey & Randolph	*Philpot St. West of Thames St.*
1831–1842	Michael Gardner	*Foot of Washington St.*
1831–1847	William F. Smith	*Philpot St. West of Thames St.*
1833–1834	Isaac H. Miles	*Philpot St. West of Thames St.*
1833–1834	Bissett	*West end Block St.*
1833–1836	Foster & Lane	*South end of Wolfe St.*
1834–1836	David Moss	*Foot of Wolfe St.*
1835–1838	Samuel Horney	*Philpot St. West of Thames St.*
1835–1838	Henry Meads	*Near Foot of Broadway*
1835–1839	James J. Williamson	*Philpot & Point Sts.*
1835–1842	Levin H. Duncan or Dunkin	*Southeast cor. Thames & Wolfe Sts.*
1837–1839	John W. Richardson	*Philpot St. West of Thames St.*
1837–1841	Solomon Mitchell	*24 Philpot Street*
1838–1854	John Auld	*Block St. near Point St.*
1840–1842	High A. Cooper	*West end of Block St.*
1840–1845	Seymour & Hunt	*Fell St. South of Thames St.*
1841–1842	Abrahams & Horstman	*Philpot St. West of Wills St.*
1842–1850	Abrahams & Cooper	*Philpot St. West of Wills St.*
1842–1866	James & Philip Muller	*Philpot & Point Sts.*
1845–1856	Hunt & Wagner	*Fell St. South of Thames St.*
1845–1857	Richardson & McKay	*N. W. cor. Wolfe & Thames Sts.*
1849–1853	Goodwin Company	*Philpot West of Thames St.*
1850–1867	J. Abrahams & Ashcroft	*S. W. cor. Philpot & Thames Sts.*
1851–1856	Sword & Matthews	*Foot of Fells St.*
1851–1864	Cooper & Butler	*Philpot & Wills Sts.*
1856–1859	George Jones	*Foot of Ann St.*
1864–1868	Cooper & Slicer	*Philpot & Wills Sts.*
1865–1869	Jones & Ashcroft	*East end of Thames St.*
1865–1888	John Wells & Sons	*Thames St. & Broadway*
1866–1950	Chesapeake Marine Rwy & DD Co.	*Philpot & Point Sts.*
1867–1882	Stevens & Newman	*Fell St. South of Thames St.*
1870–1882	Robert Ashcroft	*East end of Thames St.*
1873–1875	Malster & Donnell	*Foot of Ann St.*
1873–1887	John C. Froehlich & Co.	*Thames St.*
1876–1884	Columbian Iron Works	*Foot of Ann St.*
1882–1912	R. M. Spedden & Co.	*Thames St. & Broadway*
1887–1897	H. Brusstar & Bro.	*Philpot & Point Sts.*
1887–1898	John C. Froehlich & Co.	*Philpot & Point Sts.*

Bibliography

The Port of Baltimore in the Making,
by T. Courtenay J. Whedbee

The Story of the Baltimore & Ohio Railroad,
by Edward Hungerford

History of Baltimore City & County,
by J. Thomas Scharf (Louis H. Everts 1881)

Old Baltimore, by Annie Leakin Sioussat
(The Macmillan Co.)

Annals of Baltimore,
by Thomas W. Griffith (William Wooddy 1883)

Baltimore on the Chesapeake,
by Hamilton Owens (Doubleday, Doran & Co.)

Men of Marque,
by Cranwell and Crane (W. W. Norton & Co. Inc.)

History of the American Privateers,
by George Coggeshall (C. T. Evans, N.Y.)

Mount Vernon,
by Paul Wilstach

Sailor of Fortune,
by Hulbert Footner

The Chronicles of Baltimore,
by J. Thomas Scharf (Turnbull Bros.)

Early American Steamers,
by Erik Heyl

Baltimore Afire,
by Harold A. Williams

Greyhounds of the Sea,
by Carl C. Cutter (George Banta Co. Inc)

American Clipper Ships, Vol. I & II,
by Octavius T. Howe & Frederick C. Matthews (Argosy Antiquarian Ltd)

The Amiable Baltimoreans,
by Francis F. Beirne (E. P. Dutton & Co. Inc.)

Chesapeake Bay,
by M. V. Brewington (Bonanza Books)

Cornell's Sea Packet,
Edited by W. M. Williamson (Cornell Maritime Press)

Chesapeake Circle,
by Robert H. Burgess (Cornell Martime Press)

The Baltimore Clipper,
by Howard I. Chapelle (Tradition Press)

Fells Point Bi-Centennial Jubilee.
(The Weant Press)

CREDITS

Produced by Stanley L. Cahn
Designed by Mossman Art Studio
Typography by Modern Linotypers, Inc.
Printed by Universal Lithographers, Inc.
   on Old Forge Opaque Offset